LIVING
the
ROSARY

The Rosary's mysteries are as much about today and about your life as they are about events that happened long ago! Father John Phalen's book will help you learn to make this connection and enrich your praying of the Rosary a hundred times over.

Mitch Finley
Author of *The Rosary Handbook*

Two of my heroes are Pope John Paul II and Father Patrick Peyton, C.S.C. Both men shared an intense devotion to Our Blessed Lady and the Rosary. I know of no one who has more fully and eloquently integrated the devotion of Fr. Peyton to Mary and the luminous love for her of the pope than Father John Phalen, C.S.C. In his preaching, in his writing, in his prayer life, and in this book, he shares his own passion for Mary and her gentle way to Christ. He has a gift for relating the mysteries of the Rosary to our daily lives, and he does this better than anyone I know. I believe the readers of this book will hear echoes resounding in their own hearts of the joy, light, suffering, and glory of our Lord and his Blessed Mother, Mary.

Rev. Willy Raymond, C.S.C.
National Director
Family Theater Productions

LIVING
the
ROSARY

Finding

Your Life

in the Mysteries

JOHN PHALEN, C.S.C.

Holy Cross Family Ministries

ave maria press AmP notre dame, indiana

© 2011 by Holy Cross Family Ministries

All rights reserved. No part of this book may be used or reproduced in any manner whatsoever, except in the case of reprints in the context of reviews, without written permission from Ave Maria Press®, Inc., P.O. Box 428, Notre Dame, IN 46556.

Founded in 1865, Ave Maria Press is a ministry of the Indiana Province of Holy Cross.

www.avemariapress.com

ISBN-10 1-59471-264-6   ISBN-13 978-1-59471-264-7

Cover image © Istockphoto.com

Cover and text design by Katherine Robinson Coleman.

Printed and bound in the United States of America.

Library of Congress Cataloging-in-Publication Data

Phalen, John.

  Living the Rosary : finding your life in the mysteries / John Phalen.

    p. cm.

  Includes bibliographical references.

  ISBN-13: 978-1-59471-264-7 (pbk.)

  ISBN-10: 1-59471-264-6 (pbk.)

1. Mysteries of the Rosary. 2. Christian life--Catholic authors. I. Title.

BT303.P468 2010

242'.74--dc22

                                    2010048863

In loving memory of

John and Betty Phalen

and Servant of God Father Patrick Peyton, C.S.C.,

Educators in the Faith

Contents

3. Living the Sorrowful Mysteries

4. Living the Glorious Mysteries

Acknowledgments

I dedicate this little book to my parents, my first educators in the faith, whose commitment to family and prayer has had a profound effect on my siblings and me. They in turn were influenced by the saintly Father Patrick Peyton, whose passionate preaching about Mary and the Family Rosary lifted the spirits and the spiritual lives of millions. I thank God for such holy mentors in the faith!

I wish to thank all those who have participated in the Retreats and Missions I have been privileged to preach over the last fourteen years. They have helped me to hone these stories, and their testimony has served to convince many others of the value of finding our lives in the Mysteries of the Rosary.

Of course all those I mention in telling these stories of faith are to be thanked most sincerely as well, especially the parish communities of St. Stephen (now St. Adalbert) parish in South Bend, Indiana, and Our Lady of Good Counsel parish in Bedford-Stuyvesant, Brooklyn, where I have served; my family members, living and deceased, among them my "five favorite sisters": Betsy, Susan, Peg, Pat, and Mary Ann; and my fellow religious of the Congregation of Holy Cross.

A heart-felt thank you goes to Mr. Patrick McGowan, whose editing and advice have been invaluable, and to Ave Maria Press for their enthusiasm in bringing this work to print.

And to all I have tried to serve pastorally: You have taught me so much about the presence of Christ in your lives that it has sharpened my perception of the Christ-presence in my own. Thank you!

John Phalen, C.S.C.

Introduction

The Rosary is a much-beloved devotion, but, truth be told, it was not always appreciated as such by me. I came from a family that was very committed to the faith. For us, commitment meant saying grace before meals and praying before sleep. It meant Saturday confession and Sunday Mass, followed by a discussion of the homily over donuts. It also meant gathering in the living room, as a family, to ask God's blessing and Mary's intercession for us through praying the Rosary.

I was the youngest of three children (we were eventually seven) when praying the family Rosary became our family's practice. With a very short attention span and two sisters who rather looked forward to my antics, I did my best to subvert this particular devotion. Constant motion, making faces at my sisters, sighing from the depths as if being slain by the boredom of repetition: these were the methods with which I made the family Rosary more torture than prayer for the participants. I often succeeded in getting the practice suspended altogether—which was, of course, my goal.

Ironically, I find myself today promoting the family Rosary all over the world. Servant of God Father Patrick Peyton, C.S.C. (1909–1992), left his religious Congregation, the Congregation of Holy Cross, a Rosary ministry totally dedicated to its promotion. Encouraging families to enhance their spiritual life through the communal praying of the Rosary is the goal of Holy Cross Family Ministries today. We employ film, radio, television, the Internet, billboards, news articles, books, pamphlets, Rosary-making, Rosary distribution, national contests, a family institute, rallies, retreats, missions, and a host of other methods to get this simple message across: "The family that prays together, stays together!" Father Peyton originated this theme and dedicated his priestly life to it. This book is a testament to the continued vitality of his efforts.

Servant of God, Father Peyton

I write, as Father Peyton did, about the intersection of the Rosary and my own life experiences. I do this in order to give real-life examples of how God influences us, and how contemplating the mysteries of the Rosary can encourage us in our own faith journey. Patrick Peyton came from a poor family in County Mayo, Ireland. He was always impressed when he experienced his father leading the family in the Rosary each night. That family acknowledgment of the importance of God and the prayerful turning over of family life to God became the heart of Father Peyton's later mission.

Pat traveled to the United States and entered the Congregation of Holy Cross along with his brother Tom. Both were pleased to find themselves at Our Lady's University in Notre Dame, Indiana, and they did very well in their studies. During Pat's seminary days, however, a huge obstacle presented itself. While studying theology at Catholic University and preparing himself to become a foreign missionary, Pat became deathly ill with tuberculosis. He languished with the disease for an entire year.

The doctors told Pat to "try prayer" because the things they had been trying were not working. A fellow Irishman and former professor, Father Con Haggerty, C.S.C., chided Pat, telling him in no uncertain terms, "Mary is alive. She's a one-hundred percenter, if you believe her to be. Now pray your Rosary with absolute faith like a good Irishman! Mary will answer your prayer." Pat tried the Rosary, and after a Rosary novena he was tuberculosis-free. It was his firm belief that the Rosary had saved his life, and he retold the story all over the world.

Pat recovered completely and went on to be ordained. He founded the Family Rosary in 1942 in Albany, New York. He later became a famous radio personality, chaplain to the stars of Hollywood, and the famous "Rosary Priest" whose "Family Rosary Crusades" had him speaking in person about Mary and the family Rosary to over 28 million people around the world. His film on the life of Christ is still sought after for its dramatic quality and faithfulness to the scriptures. Such was Father Peyton's confidence in Mary. Many now pray that he will someday be declared a saint.

Living the Mysteries

Despite my own youthful distaste for the Rosary, I eventually came, like Patrick Peyton, to embrace it. How did my view of the Rosary change? Life experience made all the difference. I once thought—incorrectly—that the Rosary was totally about Mary. Now I know that at the center of this prayer is "the fruit of thy womb, Jesus!" The Rosary is a Christo-centric prayer. In its various mysteries, it recounts the life of Christ, and in Christ's life, we see our own. Mary's role is to assist in this process.

The mysteries of the Rosary can and should be lived out by every Christian. If we simply pay attention, we will see that meditating on the Rosary mysteries will help us recognize how our lives and the life of Christ (and the life of the Church) connect. Over the years, I have been privileged to share many of the stories found in this book with parish communities, prayer groups, vowed religious, and priests in places all around the world. After presenting to these groups how I have lived a particular Rosary mystery in my own life, I encourage people to talk about their own experiences of annunciation, visitation, transfiguration, carrying of the cross, and resurrection. The result has always been that people discover a strong connection between the mysteries of the Rosary as experienced by Jesus and their own life experiences. This in turn makes praying the

Rosary come alive for them in ways they did not previously imagine possible.

Our challenge as Christians is to conform our lives to Christ's. The Rosary, looked at from this perspective, becomes a great way to contemplate the life of Christ, accompanied on the journey by the one who knew him best—his Mother. Mary will always bring people to her Son. We can be sure of that. Since God came to earth in the person of Jesus Christ to teach us how to live, the more we contemplate the most important moments of his life in the mysteries, the better we will be able to discern how those same mysteries work themselves out in our own lives.

History of the Rosary

When illiterate people visited a great cathedral during the Middle Ages, they were reminded by the stained glass windows, the bas relief work, and the Stations of the Cross of all those important moments of commitment, sacrifice, love, healing, and new life in the Christian story. Gazing on the representation of the mysteries (Christmas, the wedding feast at Cana, the scourging at the pillar, Easter Resurrection), the faithful person would be encouraged to live what he or she saw in accordance with the example given by Christ. In a way, the Rosary is quite similar to a cathedral. If a great cathedral is a catechism in glass and stone, then the Rosary is a catechism of the imagination.

The Rosary has always belonged to the laity. It seems to have originated from laypeople's practice of imitating the monks in their praying the Psalms in song. Since the laity could not read, they replaced the psalms with the Our Father, a prayer given by Jesus himself and one that lent itself to easy memorization. Over time, the order of the prayers evolved into the pattern we are familiar with today: an Our Father, ten Hail Marys, and the doxology (the Glory Be) in imitation of the way the monks finished every psalm with the Trinitarian formula.

While no one knows the exact date when the Rosary as we now know it took its final shape, the form we now use came together by the fourteenth century. There is a pious tradition in which a garland of roses was fashioned by monks for those female faithful who were to be martyred. Since there were so many early martyrs, the monks began to complain that they no longer had enough time to make the garlands. Their Superior suggested that they instead offer spiritual bouquets for those who were to give their lives for the faith. There are many kinds of flowers that Christians have associated with Mary, but the most popular one is the Rose. So the name 'Rosary' was adopted for the spiritual bouquet to be offered by the laity with the help of the beads.

The beads themselves evolved from the use of stones, kept in a pouch, which allowed the monks to keep track of the psalms as they prayed them. Some monks simply tied knots in their cincture as a way of counting the prayers of the Rosary. Dominicans used the Rosary as an instrument for evangelization. It still hangs at their left side, ready like a sword as a weapon for spiritual battle.

A Scriptural Prayer

The Rosary is simultaneously a very simple prayer and a very profound one. It is also profoundly scriptural. The Rosary can be understood on many levels, depending on one's age and maturity in the spiritual life. So many of the various events in the life of Christ are true mysteries—the same is true of the major events in our own lives. Somehow, in mysterious ways, God communicates with us through our life experiences. Sharing these, we are in fact sharing faith. Living the mysteries, we express our confidence in God's ways, which are not our ways.

I always find it surprising that many who claim *sola escritura* (scripture alone) have little use for the Rosary. They obviously have not paid enough attention to the first few chapters of St. Luke's Gospel. The first words of the Hail Mary are taken from the words of the Angel Gabriel to Mary. They are followed by words from Mary's cousin, Elizabeth: "Blessed are you among women, and blessed is the fruit of your womb." No one who looks carefully at its prayers can claim that the Rosary is not scriptural.

I like to think of Mary praying the Rosary with us, as if she were relating the events in the life of her Son using a photo album. She slowly turns the pages and exclaims, "I remember this distinctly: this is where my Son was beaten mercilessly. How it broke my heart! See how he suffered for us!" Turning the pages further, Mary comes upon the Pentecost event. "We would, by tradition, stay up all night on this feast, celebrating Moses presenting the commandments. I remember so clearly when the noise came, as if a great wind, and the tongues of fire gave great courage to my Son's apostles. They were no longer fearful to evangelize. They even had new gifts of communication." Mary gently shares with us all the high points of Jesus' life and the consequences of his being among us and sacrificing his life for us.

Of course, the Our Father is the quintessential prayer, recommended by Jesus himself to the apostles and to all of us. Again, it is a most profound prayer, though simple. It is a prayer asking that God the Father's Kingdom come and that his will be done. What a different world we would have if these requests were asked for with complete sincerity! So much of the pride and greed of humanity stands in the way of this. We do not pray for riches or power or victory in the Our Father. Instead, we pray to the God who gives us "daily bread" and forgives us as we forgive others. This is the God Jesus reveals to us as Father.

In addition to the Our Father and the Hail Mary, the Rosary invites us to pray the doxology. The Scriptures reveal a Triune God (Father, Son, and Holy Spirit) as preached by Jesus himself, who came to do his Father's will and promised that the Advocate would come after him. These three prayers, the Our Father, the Hail Mary, and the Glory Be, are the heart and the essence of the

Rosary, along with the announcement of the Mystery to be contemplated with each decade. All of this is highly scriptural and deserves our attention as Christians.

Pope John Paul II and the Rosary

Rosarium Virginis Mariae, the 2002 letter from Pope John Paul II about the Rosary, has renewed interest in the ancient prayer form. This most beloved prayer of the Pope was referred to as a "compendium of the Gospel" and a means of "contemplating the face of Christ with Mary."

The Holy Father, who prayed the Rosary daily, points out in the letter:

> "It was in [Mary's] womb that Christ was formed, receiving from her a human resemblance which points to an even greater spiritual closeness. No one has ever devoted himself to the contemplation of the face of Christ as faithfully as Mary." (*RVM*, chapter 1, 10)

The Pope goes on to point out that we can learn much about Jesus' life by noticing the countenance of Mary:

> "Mary's gaze is always one of adoration and wonder, as at Jesus' birth . . .
>
> It was sometimes a questioning look, as in the finding in the Temple . . .
>
> It was a penetrating gaze, as at Cana when Mary anticipated Christ's ministry . . .

At times it was a look of sorrow, especially beneath the cross . . .

It was a gaze radiant with joy at the Resurrection at Easter . . .

It was a gaze afire with the outpouring of the Holy Spirit at Pentecost."

Mary, according to the Pope, accompanies us in the praying of the Rosary. She is the one who knew Christ best. She lived through all the mysterious events of his life. She is a proud mother who could not be more pleased than to see us draw closer to her Son and conform our lives to his by means of this simple, contemplative prayer. A good mother can communicate much to her children simply through her facial expression. We, too, can come to know Jesus Christ better at Mary's feet.

The Holy Father described the Rosary in his letter as an "exquisitely contemplative prayer." It starts with Mary's human experience, and it encourages us to learn from our own. The Rosary is . . .

- **Remembering Christ with Mary.** Through meditation on the mysteries, we make them present, much as the remembering of Jesus at Mass is making Christ present in the Eucharist.

- **Learning Christ with Mary.** This does not mean simply learning about him. It means learning him: getting to know him and his life's passion. No one knows Christ better than his Mother, who said, "Do whatever he tells you!"

- **Being conformed to Christ with Mary.** St. Paul tells us to have the mind of Christ, to "put on" Christ as one puts on a garment. Often good friends begin to look and speak like each other. Christ the friend should influence our lives this way. Mary watches over the human growth of both Christ and the Church.

- **Praying to Christ with Mary.** As St. Paul says, we do not know how to pray as we ought. Jesus, the one Mediator, is our Way of prayer. Mary, his purest reflection, shows us the way. She is all-powerful by grace.

- **Proclaiming Christ with Mary.** Others need to come to know this same Christ, perhaps through coming to know us as his faithful followers. Pastors and laity can use the Rosary as a significant evangelization tool.

The Pope asked us to pray the Rosary for peace and for families, and even quotes Servant of God Father Peyton's famous theme: "The Family that prays together stays together." Another deep insight of John Paul is that "each mystery of the Rosary, carefully meditated, sheds light on the mystery of man." He asserts that in Christ, our path is recapitulated:

- In the Joyful Mysteries, contemplating Christ's birth, we learn the sanctity of life; contemplating the household of Nazareth, we learn the original truth of the family by God's plan.

- According to the Mysteries of Light, listening to the Master's public teachings, we are enlightened to enter the Kingdom of God.

- In the Sorrowful Mysteries, following Christ to Calvary, we learn the meaning of salvific suffering.

- And according to the Glorious Mysteries, contemplating Christ and Mary in glory, we see the good toward which we are called if we allow ourselves to be healed and transformed by the Holy Spirit.

The Holy Father claims that the Rosary "marks the rhythm of human life, bringing it into harmony with the rhythm of God's own life in the joyful communion of the Holy Trinity, our life's destiny and deepest longing" (*RVM*, Chapter 2, 25). How true it is that we can find the rhythm of our own lives in the Rosary! This is really the insight upon which this whole book is based: in following the life of Christ in the mysteries of the Rosary, we find the rhythm God intends for our own lives. The contemplative praying of the Rosary can result in a deeper understanding of ourselves and the marvelous blessings we have received, almost without our acknowledging them. We can slowly come to recognize the sanctity of life and the truth of the family, the "meaning of the Kingdom of God Jesus taught," the significance of salvific suffering, and the very goal of our lives: the glory of heaven.

Repetition and Mantra

I find it somewhat frustrating that people today look almost anywhere but within their own tradition for experiences of "spirituality." Institutional religion has become a negative concept to many. I do not see it that way at all. Institutions survive over time, while movements and fads fade away. To my way of thinking, when Jesus said to Simon, "You are 'Peter' and on this 'Rock' I will build my Church," I believe he was thinking not only spiritually, but institutionally. Of course, any human institution will have its flaws. Peter himself was no golden paragon of virtue. He was, rather, an example of human weakness. And yet Jesus chose him and challenged him to feed his sheep.

Many who, after Vatican II, went looking for contemplation through "mantra" styles of prayer overlooked the tradition of praying the Rosary contemplatively. Here we have the repetition of simple prayers that lead us into a deeper reality of the life of Christ and our own lives! Repetition can be boring, or it can be profound. It depends upon how we see and use it. Call it "mantra," and it's intriguing!

The Eucharistic Liturgy itself gives us another example of prayers important enough to repeat. There is something in our psyche that recognizes that it is not enough to say, "Lord, Have Mercy!" only once. It needs repeating because it is profound. We need the Lord's mercy and forgiveness, and as we repeat the petition, we are invited to go deeper into that reality. It bears repeating several times: "Lord, have mercy, Lord, have mercy; Christ have mercy, Christ have mercy; Lord have mercy, Lord have mercy!" Six times we say it. The repetition invites us to plumb the depths of this profound and humbling prayer.

The same is true for the Holy, Holy and the Lamb of God. It is not enough to say, "God is holy," and simply carry on with the prayer of the canon. No, God is "holy, holy, holy!" Asking the Lamb of God, who by his sacrifice takes away the sins of the world, to have mercy on us is also repeated. It is profound. It bears repeating.

I look upon the Rosary the same way. It's a simple invitation given to Mary and to us, but it's profound. It bears repeating ten times over for each mystery. We repeat many things we do. Perhaps the most important is saying "I love you" to the one who is closest to us. Bishop Fulton Sheen answers those who protest about the repetition of the Rosary by asking, "How many times do you have to say 'I love you' to the one you are married to?" One simply cannot get away with, "Oh, honey, I told you last week: I love you!" Time goes on. People change. "How do you like me now?" is an important question. Jesus asked Peter three times: "Peter, do you love me?" In the Rosary, every bead answers "Yes!"

The Luminous Mysteries

When I first met the bishop of Chosica, Peru—Bishop Norbato Strotman—and he heard I was the president of Holy Cross Family Ministries, he made this observation: "We are missing mysteries about the public life of Christ. We have that life recounted in the scriptures, so why wouldn't we use this material?"

I don't know whether the bishop made this suggestion to Pope John Paul II or to then-Cardinal Ratzinger (now Pope Benedict), whom he knows very well. But, with the letter *Rosarium Virginis Mariae*, the suggestion is made that the Luminous Mysteries be added to the practice of the Rosary. My experience in traveling the world since indicates that the lay faithful, the "custodians of the Rosary," if you will, both like the suggestion and accept it.

The new mysteries make it clearer that the Rosary is, in fact, about the whole life of Christ. When there were only three sets of mysteries, we left Jesus at age twelve in the Finding in the Temple, and we picked up his life again only when he was thirty-three years old and suffering the Agony in the garden. Obviously, much had taken place in the interim! We have no trustable account of his home life, but his public life we have right there in the scriptures. Contemplating these new mysteries helps make the process of conforming our lives to Christ more complete.

Three to One

A final word about the four sets of mysteries of the Rosary: Neville Ward, in speaking to Father Peyton in his day, said life was like the mysteries of the Rosary, two to one: two events for joy to every one event for sorrow. Now, with the proportion enhanced, I find the Rosary to be as satisfying as the formula for a good Manhattan: three to one! Three parts bourbon to one part sweet vermouth, with a drop of bitters besides. And in life, one for sorrow; three for joy, with a bit of suffering besides! Sound like the rhythm of human life to you? I do think we have three times the number of joyful experiences in life as the number of sorrowful ones. If you examine your life deeply (and repeatedly), I'll bet you find this to be true for yourself as well. Try this as an examination of conscience at the end of the day: Ask what kind of day it's been: joyful, luminous, sorrowful, or glorious, and why. Here's to your fruitful reading! Don't forget to take the time to answer the reflection questions at the end of each chapter. They will help you find your life in the mysteries.

LIVING THE JOYFUL

MYSTERIES

The Annunciation:
The Message of an Angel

In the sixth month the angel Gabriel was sent by God to a town in Galilee called Nazareth, to a virgin engaged to a man whose name was Joseph, of the house of David. The virgin's name was Mary. And he came to her and said, "Greetings, favored one! The Lord is with you." But she was much perplexed by his words and pondered what sort of greeting this might be. The angel said to her, "Do not be afraid, Mary, for you have found favor with God. And now, you will conceive in your womb and bear a son, and you will name him Jesus. He will be great and will be called the Son of the Most High, and the Lord God will give to him the throne of his ancestor David. He will reign over the house of Jacob forever, and of his kingdom there will be no end."

Mary said to the angel, "How can this be, since I am a virgin?"

The angel said to her, "The Holy Spirit will come upon you, and the power of the Most High will overshadow you; therefore, the child to be born will be holy; he will be called Son of God. And now, your relative Elizabeth in her old age has also conceived a son; and this is the sixth month for her who was said to be barren. For nothing will be impossible with God."

Then Mary said, "Here am I, the servant of the Lord; let it be with me according to your word." Then the angel departed from her.

Luke 1:26–38

God (or the Angel Gabriel?) had my complete attention. The tears running down my face were making the gentleman sitting next to me on the plane a bit uncomfortable—I could tell by his shifting in his seat. An eager twenty-one-year-old traveling home, I was focusing in prayer and reflection on the few months I had just spent in Peru, working as a volunteer with God's people there. I knew that during my short stay I had not done much for Peru; I had painted a few adobe houses pastel colors, which would be sure to wear off before long. Nevertheless, I had the impression that Peru had done quite a number on me; that this experience would never wear off. It would possibly even change the course of my life! I was, to say the least, greatly troubled!

Through my tears, I recalled Mr. and Mrs. Paredes and the medical clinic they had set up just outside of Cartavio, in the Santa Rosa section, a place made up of former pig sties that many disenfranchised people now called home. They always kept up their hope amid so many signs of poverty and despair. The people suffered together, but they also knew how to celebrate together. They had inspired me to do more with my faltering

Spanish than I'd ever thought possible. Was it true that I was really communicating with people, talking about God with them, and even laughing at their jokes in a language that contained within itself an entirely different view of the world than the one I'd grown up with? "How could this be?" I thought. A new world had been opened up.

How could it be that I was stirred on the plane to sense an invitation in all this, one that scared me a bit? The "Angel" told me not to be afraid. Could God be asking me to drop all my personal plans of becoming a professor of literature after ordination and working at one of the colleges sponsored by my religious community? Could the Lord be inviting me to follow up on this intense interest I'd experienced in the Latino people? Was I meant to work with Hispanics in ministry, either in Peru or in my own country? How could all this be?

The answer was coming to me now. It could be by the power of the Holy Spirit, whose presence I had felt deeply during my visit as a volunteer. My interest in the people was a pastoral one. I was being called to minister, somehow, among Spanish-speaking people. This was clear to me. And it was also clear to me that this invitation was not due to my simple musings. It was an invitation from God, even "made known by the message of an angel," and by God's good grace it would be realized. "Nothing will be impossible with God."

The revelation given to me in that moment was overwhelming. I felt much as I had when I concluded in prayer that I would enter the seminary, because it seemed to be what God wanted of me. This, now, was a call within a call, to work with Latinos as a priest. I had vowed to be obedient to God, and here God's will was being made very clear to me. I said 'yes' and placed myself in God's hands as the plane droned homeward. In the ensuing years, I have come to know some of the beauty and the nuance of the Hispanic cultures, and have greatly enjoyed pastoral ministry with Latinos.

This may or may not strike you as an annunciation story. I am certain that it is. God has a way of announcing to us, through the "Angels," just what it is that God wills for us to do with our lives. When it happens, we know it. And though we are not full of grace or immaculately conceived, and though we do not enjoy the same level of prayerful communication with God as Mary did, we can follow her example in our initial fright, and then in our questioning for clarification, and finally in our saying, "Yes, I am the servant of the Lord. May it be done according to your word!"

Do you ever think about and pray over your annunciation stories? If you are married, think of how the Angel Gabriel made it clear to you that "this is the one to marry!" There is surely an annunciation story there. Who was your "Angel Gabriel"? What signs of God's will did you pick up on? Did you go through a process of prayer, doubt, and sleepless nights? With whom did you consult before you made your decision? Did you sense God's presence in that decision?

Or take your profession—by profession I mean whatever it is that occupies your attention, time, and energy as work (schoolwork, maintenance tasks, and housework all count!): how did you come to know that this was for you, that you had the gifts to be a nurse or a construction worker or a police officer, banker, lawyer, or teacher?

God is communicating with us right now, quite regularly, letting us know what God's will is for us. It happened this way for Mary of Nazareth, and she became the Mother of God according to God's word. It happens this way for us.

All of us want to live according to God's word as well. There is an annunciation story that is the beginning of our vocation stories. As we contemplate the annunciation that Our Lady received and accepted, we pray the first Joyful mystery of the Rosary. As we repeat the words of the Hail Mary, perhaps we can reflect on our own annunciation stories, how we came to do God's will as revealed to us by the message of an angel. For those who still have not received such revelation of what God wants of them, pray to be attentive to the message of God's angels.

There is depth to be added to our prayer relationship with the Lord here. Of course, hindsight is very helpful to us as we attempt to discern our various annunciation moments while praying the Rosary. Hopefully contemplating the mystery of God's annunciation to Mary will help us to recognize the annunciations of the same God in our own lives. May our response to such moments be as courageous and self-giving as that of Mary herself.

QUESTIONS FOR REFLECTION

Recall an annunciation you received. Did it speak to you regarding whom to marry or what profession to undertake? Something else?

Who were the various "Angels Gabriel" that were instruments of God's annunciation to you?

The Visitation:
Being Christ for One Another

In those days Mary set out and went with haste to a Judean town in the hill country, where she entered the house of Zechariah and greeted Elizabeth. When Elizabeth heard Mary's greeting, the child leapt in her womb. And Elizabeth was filled with the Holy Spirit and exclaimed with a loud cry, "Blessed are you among women, and blessed is the fruit of your womb. And why has this happened to me, that the mother of my Lord comes to me? For as soon as I heard the sound of your greeting, the child in my womb leapt for joy. And blessed is she who believed that there would be a fulfillment of what was spoken to her by the Lord." And Mary said,

> "My soul magnifies the Lord,
> and my spirit rejoices in God my Savior,
> for he has looked with favor on the lowliness
>   of his servant.
> Surely, from now on all generations will call
>   me blessed;
> for the Mighty One has done great things for
>   me,
> and holy is his name.
> His mercy is for those who fear him
> from generation to generation.

He has shown strength with his arm;
he has scattered the proud in the thoughts of
    their hearts.
He has brought down the powerful from their
    thrones,
and lifted up the lowly;
he has filled the hungry with good things,
and sent the rich away empty.
He has helped his servant Israel
in remembrance of his mercy,
according to the promise he made to our
    ancestors,
to Abraham and to his descendants for ever."

And Mary remained with her for about three
months and then returned to her home.

Luke 1:39–56

Once Mary receives the invitation to become the
Mother of the King and accepts it as the handmaid of the
Lord, she immediately goes on a long journey through
the hill country to visit her cousin, Elizabeth. Though the
scriptures do not indicate this, Mary is probably accompanied by Joseph, since the trip would be an arduous
one through dangerous territory.

Entering Zechariah's house, Mary greets Elizabeth.
Why does she go there? Perhaps because it had just
been revealed by the Angel Gabriel that the kinswoman
of Mary had conceived a son in her old age and was
already in her sixth month of child-bearing. Mary could

be a help to her elderly relatives. When the two meet, they embrace, because each is a kind of sacrament for the other, confirming that the blessing of new life they are expecting is truly a gift from God.

The child in Elizabeth's womb leaps for joy, and Elizabeth herself proclaims Mary to be "the mother of my Lord." How does she know this? Through the guidance of the Holy Spirit, who is very much present to each of these holy women. The unborn child is the first to recognize the presence of the unborn King. What a testimony for our time when the rights of the unborn are so shamelessly denied!

Mary rejoices in God her Savior, proclaiming the greatness of the Lord. "The Mighty One has done great things for me," she says. Mary has been given the vocation of being the mother of the One whose kingdom will have no end. She is all gratitude and joy that God would lift up the lowly this way, so she shares this news with her relative, who already seems to recognize this truth. We could say that Mary is bringing Christ to Elizabeth as she brings him to the world.

This is what visitation is about: bearing Christ, even being Christ for the other. At the same time, it is recognizing the Christ in the other. We have many visitations each day of our lives. If we go to the nursing home to visit someone elderly and/or sick, the challenge is to be Christ for that person, making sure she or he knows of the love of God that has been demonstrated in our love for him or her. The other challenge, at times more difficult for us since we may be visiting one who suffers great diminishment, is to recognize the Christ in the other, and rejoice in that discovery.

Often when we make visitations, "just listening" is our major task. People want to talk about their lives and experiences. People long for someone to pay attention to them and their stories, especially when their spouse is deceased or incapacitated. They need to know that someone cares enough to be there for them. Perhaps we do not have a great amount of time to spend with a particular person, but the fact that we go out of our way to make the visitation tells them of their importance in our lives. Knowing this can be life-giving for them.

Sometimes we visit someone, and others comment, "Why do you spend your precious time with that loser? He's always complaining, and he talks too much! He is so mean and self-centered!" And sometimes we respond like Sancho Panza in reference to his good friend, Don Quixote de la Mancha: "I like him! I really like him! Tear out my fingernails one by one. I like him! I don't have a very good reason. It's just that our friendship has always been in season."

Perhaps God has made each of us with just the right combination of gifts and temperament to reach people others cannot. This certainly appears to be the case in my own life. I am a firm believer that there are some people on this earth who are waiting precisely for me to spend time with them. I believe the same to be true for all of us. Sometimes the chemistry between two people simply allows them to discover the Christ in each other, and perhaps leap at the revelation. And all the while, others are mystified about how we could stand to even be in each other's presence. Visitations help us to discern who those particular people are for us. The challenge then becomes one of exercising a ministry of presence to them.

I used to visit with Doña Luciana every "Ash Friday," as we referred to it ("Viernes de Ceniza" in Spanish), the Friday after Ash Wednesday. Doña Luciana was quite elderly and had one visible tooth, which almost always appeared because she grinned a good deal of the time. She lived on the edge of a Midwestern town, where many migrant Mexican families could be found. Since Ash Wednesday was such a busy day for priests, I made a deal with this joyful elder. I would visit with her on the Friday after Ash Wednesday so that she could receive her Lenten ashes.

Our "Ash Friday" visit included talk about each of our families, the history of the area, and the difficulties of raising a family while following the migrant stream. We then took the palms from a year ago, which had been kept on the crucifix on the wall, and respectfully burned them to make the ashes. I placed the ashes on Doña Luciana's head in the Sign of the Cross, reminding her that she would return to dust. Ironically, she had been reminding me all along of my own mortality as she related the obstacles and hardships with which life had confronted her.

I always came out of Ash Friday's morning visit to Doña Luciana rejoicing. With my simple presence and appreciation of a life story, one so full of challenges met by deep faith, I was able to be Christ in some way for her. And truth be told, Doña Luciana was very much the Christ for me. Her faith had been tested more profoundly than had mine. She had been refined like gold in the fire, and though I doubt she was able to read words on a page, and though life had left her but one tooth, Doña Luciana was adept at reading my soul. She knew first-hand the kind of sacrifices and sufferings Jesus had undergone, which we tried in our small way to imitate with our Lenten penitential practices. The depth of Doña Luciana's faith always strengthened my own. The palms of Jesus' glorious entry into Jerusalem became the ashes reminding us of his death and ours. Being present to each other during "Ash Friday's" visitation helped us both, I believe, to begin Lent with hearts open to conversion and to prepare ourselves for the observances of the whole paschal mystery—the passion, death, resurrection, and ascension of the Lord.

"Just being there" counts. Whether the setting be a phone call, a text message, or an e-mail from a friend or family member looking for advice; a wake, when we do not know how to convey our sorrow or compassion (often the Rosary gives us the words); a prison or hospital where the resident or patient is tortured by thoughts of the world going by without him or her; or simply the sporting events of one's children who ask, "Did you see me get that hit, Dad? Mom?" In all these cases, our effort to accompany, listen to, and share with another amounts to time well spent.

We try with the help of God's grace to be Christ for one another as we see clearly the Christ in the other. These are moments of holy visitation, of joyful mystery. Doña Luciana has been called home to God. I look forward to a final visitation with her in the presence of Christ himself.

QUESTIONS FOR REFLECTION

Think of someone you visited—someone with whom you discovered the Christ. How was this a joyful mystery for you?

Share with someone a time when you were visited by another and the visit lifted your spirits and was just what you needed at the time.

In a given day, keep track of the number of "visitations" you have in person or by phone or internet. Ask yourself where Christ was in these visits.

The Nativity:
God Has Come Down

In those days a decree went out from Emperor Augustus that all the world should be registered. This was the first registration and was taken while Quirinius was governor of Syria. All went to their own towns to be registered. Joseph also went from the town of Nazareth in Galilee to Judea, to the city of David called Bethlehem, because he was descended from the house and family of David. He went to be registered with Mary, to whom he was engaged and who was expecting a child. While they were there, the time came for her to deliver her child. And she gave birth to her firstborn son and wrapped him in bands of cloth, and laid him in a manger, because there was no place for them in the inn.

Luke 2:1–7

Now the birth of Jesus the Messiah took place in this way. When his mother, Mary, had been engaged to Joseph, but before they lived together, she was found to be with child from the Holy Spirit. Her husband Joseph, being a righteous man and unwilling to expose her to public disgrace, planned to dismiss her quietly. But just when he had resolved to do this, an angel of the Lord appeared to him in a dream and said, "Joseph, son of David, do not be afraid to take Mary as your wife, for the child conceived in her is from the Holy Spirit. She will bear a son, and you are to name him Jesus, for he will save his people from their sins."

Matthew 1:18–21

He was in the world, and the world came into being through him; yet the world did not know him. He came to what was his own, and his own people did not accept him. But to all who received him, who believed in his name, he gave power to become children of God, who were born not of blood or of the will of the flesh or of the will of man, but of God. And the Word became flesh and lived among us, and we have seen his glory, the glory as of a father's only son, full of grace and truth.

John 1:10–14

The Lord God became one of us! This is an amazing mystery: the Incarnation. God emptied himself, so the hymn in Philippians 2 indicates, and took on all the characteristics of the human life we know so well: a life with its joyful, even ecstatic celebrations, as well as its sorrowful, even tragic moments. Jesus was born among us as a human being, poor and yet with great potential; helpless and so protected by Joseph; hungry and so nourished by Mary. Yet his glory was sung by the angels and recognized by the shepherds, themselves as poor as the King they honored. This was a child of the promise, the Messiah, the King, however disguised as a poor babe born in a stable. God had elected to send his only begotten Son to be one of us and experience all we do as humans except sin. He came to teach us to love God and one another.

Whenever we are overwhelmed by the messiness of life, by its hurts and disappointments, and whenever we are surprised by its vitality and people's ability to carry on in the face of poverty, oppression, or hardship, we can think of our brother, Jesus, and all he endured in his life. He who knew no sin was made sin for us. He came unto his own, and his own received him not. People were drawn to him, and yet the religious authorities of his time sought to trip him up in his speech. He spoke with authority and preached a message of mercy and love. His presence had a healing effect upon others. All this was quietly present as potential in the babe in the manger in Bethlehem. Generation after generation has been inspired by the scene of the Christmas crèche.

The Nativity, the third joyful mystery of the Rosary, speaks of hope in a newborn child whose presence in the world makes such a difference. All newborn children are meant to make a difference. All unborn children are meant to see the light of day. They have so much to give, so much to contribute to society. They are blessings, these children of the promise, and their arrival in the family changes the chemistry in the family completely. When asked about their moment closest to Christ, many parents speak of the moment of the birth of their child.

I come from a family of seven siblings. I am number three and the first male. This means that I had two older sisters who seemed to be rather in charge of my life in the early years. They were bigger and stronger than I was, and I considered this a challenge. When I was four years old and my mother was going to the hospital to "get" another baby (at the time I thought of it much like going to the store to get a bunch of bananas!), I prayed with great sincerity for a baby brother. After all, I was outnumbered. It was two to one. With a brother, carefully tutored by yours truly, I could even the contest between sisters and brothers and even the sides.

Who came back bundled up from the hospital looking "cute as a button"? My next sister, Peg! I was frustrated to say the least. I tried to ignore this little child, but she was entirely too cute and deserving of all the "oohs and aahs" she received. So I decided I would tutor her as if she were a boy anyway. I grew up more or less "in charge" of my younger sister's life, just as my older sisters seemed to have been "in charge" of mine. And just as I had been forced to attend too many boring tea parties, Peg was forced to learn to climb trees, sneak up on people in the forest (for training this precious skill I even charged her a nickel!), and play sports, especially basketball!

I loved basketball most of all and so needed a worthy opponent. My protégé, Peg, was to discover that she was "a good shot." I taught her everything I knew and a few things I simply made up about basketball. She responded well and represented the Philadelphia 76ers to my brilliant portrayal of the dominant Celtics of the Bill Russell years! Peg never complained about losing so many championship games, but then neither did Wilt Chamberlain!

Fast forward many years to when Peg and her boyfriend were attending a Chicago Bulls game in the Michael Jordan era. They were getting serious about each other and having a great time at the game. During a time-out, an announcement was made that all the ladies in the house were invited to compete with one another shooting foul shots at halftime. Peg knew she was good at this, so she entered the contest and won a beautiful jacket with the Bulls' insignia on the back and the words "Champion Bull Shooter!" beneath the logo. While Peg's boyfriend coveted the jacket, she insisted that it be sent to me, her brother and basketball mentor, without whose cajoling (bull shooting?) she never would have proven to be such a star.

Peg changed our life as a family by her arrival on the scene in more ways than one, and so did three more siblings in their due time. Eye has not seen, ear has not heard what God has ready for those who love Him. Each new life comes with great potential and changes all the relationships within the family.

So God has come down to become one of us, and this has changed the history of the world! We are all the better because of this great mystery. And if Jesus' coming among us is so significant, then so, too, is the coming among us of any brother or sister, be they rich or poor, beautiful or not so, expected or a complete surprise package. Our human race is constantly being renewed by the God who loves us.

But Jesus' coming among us renews us in a special way. We are to conform our life to his. As he forgave sinners, so we are to forgive those who sin against us. As he taught with authority, so we wish to speak the Gospel with an integrity that approximates his. As he brought healing into the lives of the sick, so we wish to convey God's healing power and even cast out demons by the authority of our witness to the faith.

Think of how any new life in the family has changed your way of thinking, working, being. If this is true, then think of the difference it makes that God did not leave us alone here on this earth to figure out how much He loves us. God has come down to be one of us, to try on the festal garment and sometime straightjacket of humanity. And that has made all the difference.

QUESTIONS FOR REFLECTION

Recall a time when a new life coming into your group, class, club, or family has made a real difference. Share this with a friend.

What would you say of the human potential of a baby many months incarnated in the womb to a mother considering an abortion? How would you help her move toward bringing the child to term?

While there are many nativities, only one is the Nativity of the Savior of the world, the God-man,

Jesus Christ. What does God's taking on our human nature say to you about the dignity of every human being?

The Presentation: Offering to God What God Has First Given to Us

When the time came for their purification according to the law of Moses, they brought him up to Jerusalem to present him to the Lord (as it is written in the law of the Lord, "Every firstborn male shall be designated as holy to the Lord"), and they offered a sacrifice according to what is stated in the law of the Lord, "a pair of turtle-doves or two young pigeons."

Now there was a man in Jerusalem whose name was Simeon; this man was righteous and devout, looking forward to the consolation of Israel, and the Holy Spirit rested on him. It had been revealed to him by the Holy Spirit that he would not see death before he had seen the Lord's Messiah. Guided by the Spirit, Simeon came into the temple; and when the parents brought in the child Jesus to do for him what was customary under the law, Simeon took him in his arms and praised God, saying,

"Master, now you are dismissing your servant
    in peace,
according to your word;
for my eyes have seen your salvation,

which you have prepared in the presence of all
   peoples
a light for revelation to the Gentiles
and for glory to your people Israel."

And the child's father and mother were amazed at what was being said about him. Then Simeon blessed them and said to his mother, Mary, "This child is destined for the falling and the rising of many in Israel, and to be a sign that will be opposed so that the inner thoughts of many will be revealed—and a sword will pierce your own soul, too."

There was also a prophet, Anna, the daughter of Phanuel of the tribe of Asher. She was of a great age, having lived with her husband for seven years after her marriage, then as a widow to the age of eighty-four. She never left the temple but worshipped there with fasting and prayer night and day. At that moment she came and began to praise God and to speak about the child to all who were looking for the redemption of Jerusalem.

When they had finished everything required by the law of the Lord, they returned to Galilee, to their own town of Nazareth. The child grew and became strong, filled with wisdom; and the favor of God was upon him.

Luke 2:22–35

"I know of one very special birthday that we all want to acknowledge: Sam Nightengale turns eighty today. Sam, please stand and be recognized!" A smiling

African American gentleman stood and acknowledged the applause. Dressed in a beautiful gray suit and colorful tie, this amiable elder looked a great deal like Nelson Mandela. The community gathered for Sunday Mass expressed their appreciation for him with thunderous clapping.

I loved celebrating Mass with this African American community of Brooklyn. It was so joyful and inclusive. People dressed as if this was the most important event of the week—because it was! And they truly supported each other.

On that particular day, however, my enthusiasm came crashing down around me when one musician spoke with me after Mass. To my surprise, he was steaming angry about how I had presented the man celebrating his birthday. "You have lots to learn about pastoring a black congregation, Father! You never call any adult just by their first name in public. He is 'Mr. Nightengale' to us, an octogenarian, and he ought to have that respect from you too! When you say, 'Please stand up, Sam,' everybody cringes. The butler on the plantation was known as just 'Sam.' We're not slaves now, so the elders of the community all deserve titles and the use of their last name. He is never anyone less than '*Mr.* Nightengale,' and you don't present African American adults by simply using their first name! How could you do that?!"

However painful it was to receive this reproach, I had to admit it was a good lesson about presentation. The very same African Americans who dressed to the nines every Sunday spoke to each other using titles:

"Miss Lucy, how are you today?" "Officer Kearns, always a pleasure to see you, sir." I had not picked up on this formal style when I was assigned to be a white pastor of a predominantly black parish. But the people were teaching me about their customs, their history, and their backgrounds. Believe me; I have never since called an adult member of the African American community simply by his or her first name in public.

Mary and Joseph bring their child to the temple to present him to God, to give thanks, and to offer a simple sacrifice. There they meet not only God, to whom the child is consecrated, but two respected elders of the community: Simeon, who was told he would live to see the one who would bring salvation; and Anna, a prayerful widow who fasted and prayed in the Temple daily. Both have wonderful observations to make about this young child. He will be a light for the world and the glory of the people of Israel. Many will fall and rise because of him. Anna and Simeon speak so highly of Jesus that Mary and Joseph would come to expect great things of him. Simeon lets Mary know that she will have to undergo hardship because of the child, as well: "A sword will pierce your heart!"

There are very great expectations of this child involved here. He will be the Messiah and the fall and rise of many in Israel. The message is clear. He is the child of the promise, the one expected by many generations. The elders lived to see this moment, and they praised God. Great things will come of his birth among us. Our lives will be changed.

Of course, all presentations to the Lord are simply acknowledgments of blessings first received from the Lord. God is good and would have sent Jesus to be our Savior even if there were very few of us on the Earth. The love of God for us is boundless. We hope to be a reflection of that love when we attempt to present a brother or sister to someone else.

"Here he is, the old man: the drunk!" or "Here she is, the wife, the gossip queen of the neighborhood!" are obviously *not* good presentations. As in the culinary arts, our social lives demand a positive presentation. Consider how this sounds as a presentation when, as pastor, I visited a family: "Hello, Father. You just sit down here, and I'll get Danny. Maybe you can straighten him out. Here he is now, Father. Danny, say hello to Father. Father, I don't know what I'm going to do with this fellow! He's getting terrible grades in school. He teases the girls in his class. He plays hooky. He lies to us. What should I do about him, Father?"

Of course, while all these negative things are being said about him, Danny is trying to melt into the ground, he is so embarrassed. This is the first time I am meeting him. What a way for me to learn what Danny is like, with his own mother reciting for me his sins! I usually interrupt at this point, once I see what is going on, and plead, "Please, Mrs. Jones, tell me something good about Danny here. What does he do well? What qualities or virtues does he have? How do his friends think of him?"

To present someone to others requires that we look at the positive side. What is exciting and life-giving about meeting this person? What does the person have to offer to a relationship? How has God blessed him or her in special ways? Maybe I needed to ask Danny's grandparents about him in order to get some positive comments. It is sad to encounter parents putting their own children down and expressing the lowest possible expectations of their child. If his own parents think he will never amount to anything, then most likely this prophecy will be self-fulfilling. Young people especially need those closest to them to believe in them.

How did Mary and Joseph come away from this presentation of the child Jesus in the temple? They must have been delighted to hear such wonderful comments about Jesus, the child of the promise. There was a confirmation here of the significance of this particular life and how it could somehow change the history of the world. I imagine that both felt their prayer life confirmed and the promise given by the Angel Gabriel to Mary restated with assurance. The child was meant to fulfill the promise of God. In presenting him for consecration to God, it was recognized that he himself was a gift of God, shared with this faithful couple and with all God's people. The presentation was done in a most favorable light.

But there was also a touch of sadness, even in the midst of joy. Mary's heart would be pierced with a sword that the thoughts of many hearts would be laid bare. Mary in that moment could not have realized what this prediction meant. But she must have guarded in her heart a frightful premonition. She would eventually undergo great suffering. She would need the grace of God to endure it. Sometimes the gifts of God, so real and promising, require great sacrifice of God's loyal followers. The thoughts to be laid bare might be the ambivalent thoughts of Pilate, concerned about keeping his power. They might have been the thoughts of the Temple leaders, who found in Jesus a scandal and stumbling block, a challenge to their authority. His presence and action among the people contradicted their style, and so it would be better for one to sacrifice his life for the people. Those who wanted to cling to the law and the authority it gave them would need Jesus and the challenge he represented out of the way. He blasphemed, speaking as if he were God. He would have to die, and this, too, would pierce the heart of his mother.

Trusting in the providence of God would be difficult and heart-rending when it came. But for now, Joseph and Mary were content to know of the significance of the child's life. They offered back to God the one whose existence was a gift to them. They would care for him and raise him to be faithful to God in all things. The Spirit's guidance of this holy family was confirmed at the presentation in the temple.

QUESTIONS FOR REFLECTION

....

How would you present your spouse or your close friend to a visiting dignitary? Practice a positive presentation.

Knowing that there are heartaches to endure in the raising of any child, would you want to know about them in detail beforehand or not? Give reasons for your preference.

The Finding in the Temple: Doing the Work of My Father

Now every year his parents went to Jerusalem for the festival of the Passover. And when he was twelve years old, they went up as usual for the festival. When the festival was ended and they started to return, the boy Jesus stayed behind in Jerusalem, but his parents did not know it. Assuming that he was in the group of travelers, they went a day's journey. Then they started to look for him among their relatives and friends. When they did not find him, they returned to Jerusalem to search for him. After three days they found him in the temple, sitting among the teachers, listening to them and asking them questions. And all who heard him were amazed at his understanding and his answers. When his parents saw him they were astonished; and his mother said to him, "Child, why have you treated us like this? Look, your father and I have been searching for you in great anxiety."

He said to them, "Why were you searching for me? Did you not know that I must be in my Father's house?" But they did not understand what he said to them. Then he went down with them and came to Nazareth and was obedient to them. His mother treasured all these things in her heart. And Jesus increased in wisdom and in years, and in divine and human favor.

Luke 2:41–52

Jesus is with his family when the Feast of the Passover is celebrated. Probably the whole extended family has arrived in Jerusalem by caravan. The twelve-year-old must have been fascinated by the crowds and interested in learning more about the Scriptures. The returning caravan was on its way for a full day before Mary and Joseph discovered that Jesus was not with any of the family members. He must have been inadvertently left behind in the big city! If you have ever lost your child in a big department store, you know the panic that can set in. The mind starts racing and imagining the worst. Mary must have thought of all that was said of the child in the annunciation and the presentation. He is the child of the promise. He will be the cause of the rise and fall of many! His reign will never end! But he is lost!

Was he lost, or were they the ones who were lost? Perhaps they lost for a while the confidence and trust in God's providential guidance of events, which they usually enjoyed. For three days (like the three days in the tomb) the couple searched, pleading for God's help. I like to think that, searching everywhere to no avail, they were driven to the temple because of their need to pray. "O God, please help us find him! We promise never to let him out of our sight again until he is grown!" could have been their prayer. "Crisis prayer" can easily spring up out of anyone's throat when one feels that matters are out of control! If you were brought up praying the Rosary, then often the crisis prayer takes the form of a quick decade. In such a case, this mystery of the finding would be the most important decade to pray.

The faithful Jewish couple enters the Temple to pray, and there he is; the child, Jesus, having a deep conversation with the elders about the scriptures. They are amazed at his grasp of the area of which they are considered the experts. There follows an exchange perhaps familiar to all of us: "Why have you done this to us? Your father and I were in anguish looking for you!" says Mary. Jesus responds: "Did you not know that I must be in my Father's house?" (Some translations say: "about the work of my Father?") This may indicate a realization on his part concerning who his Father is, and it certainly indicates a commitment to do the will of the Father, something his mother had agreed to and something he himself would preach, pray for, and struggle humanly with in his agony and crucifixion. The scene ends with the boy Jesus returning home with Mary and Joseph to Nazareth to be obedient to them. Mary treasured all these things in her heart.

When does the Finding in the Temple happen in our everyday lives? Actually, Jesus seems to be finding out something about what his Father expects of him. He is discovering what the purpose of his life is. He must be about the work and the will of his Father, even if that might cause conflict.

I remember when I was a pastor of a parish in Bedford-Stuyvesant, Brooklyn, in the late '80s and early '90s. There was a teenager in the parish who was showing an interest in graffiti, something which was not appreciated by the rest of the parishioners. Who was defacing the bathroom walls? What would motivate someone to do such a thing? A name was reported to me.

Well, it just so happened that right around this time, I was called to officiate at a very unusual wake service. It was the wake of a seventeen-year-old graffiti artist! He had wiped out the "tag," the signature of another graffiti artist, on a building, and the other teen had stabbed him with a knife and taken his life. I contacted the teenager from my parish and invited him to accompany me to this wake service. He came along, very curious.

When we arrived, we both got the impression that graffiti was the real religion of most of the people present at the funeral home. There were two large sheets of cardboard right next to the coffin, where people had signed their tags to indicate their presence at the wake. Many photos of the buildings the deceased had "enhanced" by his artwork were placed in the coffin, leaning against the lid. As I tried to preach from a Christian perspective about the death of this young man and people's yearning for eternal life, the blank stares of the mourners made me think, "Christianity is foreign to them." The parents were showing great pride in their son's work, recalling the risks he had taken to paint his message on various buildings, trains, and bridges. They seemed to consider him a kind of martyr to graffiti as a way of life.

The young man from my parish took it all in, and as we were driving home he said, "I couldn't believe that they had left a spray paint can in his coffin." We were both saddened by the fact that the young seventeen-year-old had not found more constructive ways to use his considerable talents, and I knew then that at least in this case, our parish graffiti problem was over with. Someone had been shaken by what we had witnessed. You could say he had been convinced to find healthier ways to express his artistic ability. Seeing how his own life could possibly end, he chose another, saner path. He found a way to be in his Father's house without altering its decor.

I once had a kind of "finding" moment of my own. I owe so much to my parents, God rest them, especially since they taught me the faith. I knew them to be hard-working and self-sacrificing Catholics who were very committed to their religion and to their family. We sometimes prayed the family Rosary together. Two of my father's brothers were Jesuit priests and my parents had responded positively to my interest in the religious life and priesthood.

Sadly, as it became clearer to me that the Lord was calling me to work with different ethnic groups, folks our family had never had much contact with, it became clear that my family was not altogether approving. I didn't condemn them for this. I tend to chalk up the clannishness of the Irish Americans to the experience of the famine in Ireland that forced them to emigrate and the terrible bias they encountered when they arrived in the United States. They had to stick together if they were to get jobs and enjoy security for their families. Insulting nicknames were often used for various ethnic groups, as we were always encouraged to "stick to our own kind."

I decided that I was not going to stick to my own kind, and as I pursued working with Hispanics and blacks from many nations, my encounter with my parents about it was difficult—for all involved. I did not want to confront the very people who had been such good examples of Catholicism for me. But it bothered me greatly that the teaching that we are all equal in the sight of God, all sons and daughters of God, was not always respected and practiced. "Why go there? Why get involved with them? Don't your own have needs too?" "Yes, but not as great a need." I was professing that I wanted to be about the work of my Father. I was already in the seminary, and I wanted my parents' support for my ministry to other ethnic groups. We worked it out in the end, and my family supported me, even if it wasn't something they were initially inclined to do. While I don't wish to claim that my motives were as pure as Jesus', this experience really was something akin to being found in the temple. I had to look my somewhat shocked parents in the eye and let them know that while obedience to them and respect for what they stood for was very important to me, being about the work of the Father was even more important. In time it became apparent to all that I was in my Father's house, albeit with plenty more to learn about how to do his work there.

We can all be "found in the temple" at various times in our lives. We can all discover the will of the Father for us, which may outweigh the advice of many who are closest to us. Obedience to the word of God is the most important obedience: hearing that word and putting it into practice the way Mary and Jesus did. When this kind of finding takes place, we always "treasure it in the heart!"

QUESTIONS FOR REFLECTION

Describe a time when you were lost, perhaps to the faith, and then found. If this does not apply to you, describe the experience of someone else you know with the "Lost and Found" of faith.

When did you ever have to be about the work of your Father despite the differing expectations of others? Describe the experience.

LIVING THE LUMINOUS

MYSTERIES

The Baptism in the Jordan: This Is My Beloved Son

Then Jesus came from Galilee to John at the Jordan, to be baptized by him. John would have prevented him, saying, "I need to be baptized by you, and do you come to me?"

But Jesus answered him, "Let it be so now; for it is proper for us in this way to fulfill all righteousness." Then he consented.

And when Jesus had been baptized, just as he came up from the water, suddenly the heavens were opened to him, and he saw the Spirit of God descending like a dove and alighting on him. And a voice from heaven said, "This is my Son, the Beloved, with whom I am well pleased."

Matthew 3:13–17

John the Baptist baptized with a baptism of repentance. People sought him out in the wilderness to confess their sins and receive this baptism. It was all about turning from sin and conversion of heart. John was preparing the way for the one who would come after him. This Messiah would baptize "not with water but with the Holy Spirit!"

When Jesus came to him to be baptized, John thought the roles should be reversed, that the one unworthy to tie the other's sandal strap should be the one baptized. But Jesus counseled that the Father wanted it otherwise. As Jesus came up from the water, the heavens opened, the Holy Spirit was made present in the form of a dove, and the voice of the Father said, "This is my beloved Son, in whom I am well pleased!" What a manifestation of who Jesus was! What an expression of the love that existed in the unity of Father, Son, and Spirit that made its presence felt in that moment! Perhaps no one there was totally conscious of what was happening. God himself was revealing the identity of his only-begotten Son and expressing his delight. Surely this was a significant moment, one worth remembering—it had everything to do with Jesus' identity and his importance to the Father.

Henry Nouwen, the famous spiritual writer, struggled mightily with the words of the Father concerning Jesus: "This is my beloved Son, in whom I am well pleased." He asked himself, "Where have I heard these words? Can I believe them being spoken of me by the Father?" His point was that this sentiment is most important to the spiritual welfare of one who is called to live the Gospel. If we are to know deep down in our hearts that God loves us as a Father, it helps if this message is frequently conveyed by our earthly fathers.

This is a good area for us to think about. In my case, I'm from a strongly united Irish American family. This was, in many ways, a deeply joyous and love-filled background to be from. In some ways, however, the sense of being "beloved" was not always as apparent as I would have liked. When I was five years old, for example, I was no longer kissed good-night by my father. This was something I greatly missed at first, since my sisters always received a good-night kiss. What was wrong with me? Was I chopped liver? But I eventually accepted it as part of the Irish mores: men simply did not kiss each other, and I was now being considered a man. A little man, to be sure, but a man! The trouble was that this little man could have used a few more signs of manly affection.

Later in life, I was working as a pastor in a parish in Bedford-Stuyvesant, Brooklyn, and we often had folks stop by to drop off canned food or toys that could be shared with those in the neighborhood who needed them. One family I'd known a long time had three sons, all policemen or firemen. I remember one day going out to the car of one of the police officers. He was dropping something off for the parish, as he'd done before. We hugged and he planted a quick kiss on my cheek. I tried not to let on that this really stunned me. This was an Italian family, and that was the way the men greeted each other. I remember being fascinated by the difference between the cultures.

Thinking about this incident afterward, I realized that my brother had been treated the same way by my dad: never being kissed by him after age five. When my brother died tragically at age twenty-three, the whole family was in deep grief. I remember seeing my father at the wake lovingly bend over the coffin and kiss my

brother's corpse on the face. It struck me as out of character for my dad. This was the moment in which the
words came to me: "This is my beloved Son, in whom
I am well pleased!" Different people have different
ways of saying it, of course. My dad, like many Irish-
men, would be inclined to say it by deeds rather than
words. So I knew it was true. Still, I felt deeply consoled
and loved by my earthly dad when I saw him kiss my
brother's corpse that day. The love was real, and greater
than any cultural norms limiting its expression. And I
knew with a greater certainty that Dad felt that same
love for me.

Knowing that we are loved is a huge part of our
spiritual, physical, and emotional health. Peter is asked
three times in the Resurrection story, "Do you love me?"
"Of course I do!" says the first of the apostles, who had
denied the Lord three times. "Then feed my lambs,"
says the Redeemer. The exchange happens also three
times. Real love is demonstrated in *service*, as the fifth
Luminous Mystery will re-emphasize.

The baptism of John was one of repentance. Jesus
took upon himself our sins in undergoing this baptism,
since he had no sins of his own. "He who knew no sin
became sin for us" (2 Cor 5:21). This is certainly a deed of
love. "There is no greater love than this: that one should
lay down his life for his friend" (Jn 15:13). Both baptist
and baptized would lay down their lives for preaching
this repentance and love. In both cases love is expressed
in sacrifice: the ultimate sacrifice!

Where have you heard the message "You are my beloved daughter or son. In you I am well pleased"? The message may have come from your parents or guardian, or perhaps from someone else whose love is most significant to you. The message here in this first Luminous Mystery is from God and is directed right to you. So much of our security comes from the confidence of being loved. How important to us is this message directly from the Creator? "I have loved you with an everlasting love. I have called you, and you are mine," says the Jesuit hymn.

When praying this mystery, I suggest you recall the experience of Jesus and John at the moment of Jesus' Baptism. John becomes aware that "he must increase and I must decrease" (Jn 3:30). Don't we learn the same? Jesus hears the clear message that he is the beloved of his Father. This gives him the strength to enter the process that will lead to the hour of his ultimate suffering. This is a message from God, which our hearts long to hear as well. It can give us the confidence to face whatever challenges life deals us. Whether through a kiss, a hug, or a deed of self-sacrifice, this Mystery concerns God's message of love directed at Jesus Christ and at all of us as God's children. Prayer is sometimes just enjoying the fact that God is so pleased with us!

QUESTIONS FOR REFLECTION

Describe a time when you heard the words, "You are my beloved son/daughter in whom I am well pleased."

How has God made His divine love for you evident in your life recently?

The Wedding Feast at Cana: Do Whatever He Tells You!

On the third day there was a wedding in Cana of Galilee, and the mother of Jesus was there. Jesus and his disciples had also been invited to the wedding. When the wine gave out, the mother of Jesus said to him, "They have no wine."

And Jesus said to her, "Woman, what concern is that to you and to me? My hour has not yet come."

His mother said to the servants, "Do whatever he tells you."

Now standing there were six stone water-jars for the Jewish rites of purification, each holding twenty or thirty gallons. Jesus said to them, "Fill the jars with water." And they filled them up to the brim. He said to them, "Now draw some out, and take it to the chief steward." So they took it.

When the steward tasted the water that had become wine and did not know where it came from (though the servants who had drawn the water knew), the steward called the bridegroom and said to him, "Everyone serves the good wine first, and then the inferior wine after the guests have become drunk. But you have kept the good wine until now."

Jesus did this, the first of his signs, in Cana of
Galilee, and revealed his glory; and his disciples
believed in him.

John 2:1–11

Many of the Luminous Mysteries make reference to
the Sacraments of the Church. The first spoke of Baptism. This one treats Marriage. There was a wedding
feast at Cana. Jesus and his disciples were there, and
so was Mary, his mother. The festivities, which in those
days probably lasted a whole week and involved many
people, were going well. Then Mary noticed that the
wine had run out. Like a good Jewish mother, she talked
to her Son about it. "They have no wine," she said. His
response can perhaps sound stern to us today. "Woman,
what concern is that to you and to me? My hour has
not yet come." To some theologians, the mention of
"woman" implies a whole theology of Mary as the new
Eve, the first woman. The "hour" is that of Jesus' passion, death, resurrection, and ascension (all mysteries
of the Rosary). Mary does not tell her Son what to do.
Rather she says to the servers, "Do whatever he tells
you."

We all know the rest of the story: how Jesus told
the servers to fill six stone jars with water (around
150 gallons, perhaps signifying the abundance of God's
grace). Once this was done, Jesus directed that they draw
some of the liquid out and take it to the steward. They
did so, and the steward tasted it and praised the couple
for saving the "good wine" for later in the celebration.

The water had become wine, and Jesus' disciples began to believe in him. The whole incident, the scriptures tell us, revealed his glory.

Marriage is the sacrament performed by the two people it affects the most: the husband and the wife. Do they ever get to turn water into wine? Perhaps not, but they can turn their love for each other into children, incarnations of God's love. Life with their children will teach them all about loving self-sacrifice.

Christian marriage is the starting point of a life-long intimate relationship, which hopefully will make each person more authentic and more loving. Like so many efforts backed by good intentions, it yields what you put into it with the help of God's grace. "A wedding is a day; a marriage is a lifetime." Too many couples are seemingly more concerned about the wedding than the marriage. One wonders at times whether the couple realizes that they are meant to be blessings for each other for the rest of their lives. Their love is to be a seeking of the good of the other and a dedication to the children, if God gives them children, also for a lifetime. Yet the crisis at the wedding is less likely to be the wine running out. If anything, there will be way more alcoholic beverages available than necessary or appropriate. The problem might be that the stretch limo could not maneuver the corner, or that the bride is so nervous about how the day will go that she shows up an hour late to meet her groom, who though he is relieved not to have been "stood up" is still perspiring profusely all during the ceremony. Sometimes during the ceremony,

I repeat to myself the words of Jesus from the cross as the newlyweds march down the aisle: "Father, forgive them, for they know not what they do!"

How can one replicate Jesus' miracle at Cana? Perhaps by encouraging the couple to breathe, to concentrate on the readings and the message, and to be conscious when the vows are pronounced. At least that is what I sense Mary to mean as she tells me: "Do whatever he tells you!" Paradoxically, another way of replicating the miracle is to wait on marriage until one can be more certain that the "hour" has indeed come!

Once, a couple from South Bend, Indiana, came to me to prepare for their marriage. It took a couple of sessions before I realized that there was a baby already on the way. I advised them (as I always feel obligated to do in such situations), "You might consider separating these two events: the welcoming of a child, an innocent life, into this world appropriately, and the matter of your marriage to each other," I said. "Why not avoid the rush to make it all right in the eyes of the world by a quick wedding before the birth? What if, in a moment of heated argument, you were to say to your spouse: 'I only married you because of the child anyway!' Even if untrue, once said, these words cannot be taken back, and they are very hurtful words. They would almost certainly cause your spouse to doubt your real commitment to the marriage. Perhaps you might consider welcoming the child and suspending your plans for marriage for a while. Keep going together, and if God wants it, you will be back to continue planning a marriage afterward." The couple went home to think it over.

Most often, when a couple wishes to be married before a first child is due, their response to my concerns is, "We understand. When is the soonest date possible to get married, Father?" But this couple was different. They returned saying they had talked it out, and they would suspend the marriage plans in order to welcome the baby. The mother would raise the child, and the father would assist economically and by visiting frequently with the child. Something like a year later, the couple was ready to continue with their marriage preparation.

Years later, I ran into the couple again. They had moved to a city in the southwest, and when they heard I was going to give a talk there, they came to see me. They were all gratitude that I had helped them make solid decisions. Their two daughters were happy and well-adjusted. Other teens would come to this couple looking for advice, they told me. It seems they trusted these two to have some wisdom about life decisions. I knew they were right. They never allowed the early birth of their first child to become an issue between them. The absence of blame made for an abundance of love.

What does all this have to do with the wedding feast at Cana? There is a wedding, and a crisis has happened. Jesus' presence amidst this crisis brings relief and joy. When we pray this second Luminous Mystery of the Rosary, let us think not only of the couple Jesus helped through the intercession of his mother. Let us think of weddings we witness and implore the grace of God to be as effective in the lives of the newlyweds.

Jesus is revealing his glory even today in the midst of marriages. And more and more of God's people are finding their belief in him deepened thereby.

QUESTIONS FOR REFLECTION

Think of a marriage you witnessed recently. How would you pray that Jesus would bless it?

What elements of our culture work against life-long faithfulness in marriage?

The Proclamation
of the Kingdom:
The Power of Forgiveness

Then some people came, bringing to Jesus a paralyzed man, carried by four of them. And when they could not bring him to Jesus because of the crowd, they removed the roof above him; and after having dug through it, they let down the mat on which the paralytic lay. When Jesus saw their faith, he said to the paralytic, "Son, your sins are forgiven."

Now some of the scribes were sitting there, questioning in their hearts, "Why does this fellow speak in this way? It is blasphemy! Who can forgive sins but God alone?"

At once Jesus perceived in his spirit that they were discussing these questions among themselves; and he said to them, "Why do you raise such questions in your hearts? Which is easier, to say to the paralytic, 'Your sins are forgiven,' or to say, 'Stand up and take your mat and walk'? But so that you may know that the Son of Man has authority on earth to forgive sins"—he said to the paralytic—"I say to you, stand up, take your mat and go to your home."

And he stood up and immediately took the mat and went out before all of them so that they were all amazed and glorified God, saying, "We have never seen anything like this!"

Mark 2:3–12

Forgiveness is at the heart of the Christian message. The kingdom Christ preached was, after all, a kingdom of justice, love, peace, and forgiveness. Jesus even forgave those who killed him. How many times must we forgive? Seventy times seven! In other words, "always!"

Pope John Paul II, when he suggested the new Luminous Mysteries, chose Mark 2:3–12 as his reference point for this mystery. Here a paralytic is brought in by his friends and lowered through the roof of a packed house right in front of Jesus. And Jesus says to him: "Your sins are forgiven." The people begin to murmur against him: "Who but God can forgive sins? He blasphemes!" The response: "But that you may know that the Son of Man has authority to forgive sins on earth," he said to the paralytic, "I say to you, arise, take your mat and go home." The kingdom preached is a kingdom of forgiveness.

This Mystery of the Rosary is perhaps the most expansive of them all. It would include the Sermon on the Mount, the Beatitudes, all the Parables (beginning as they do with "The Kingdom of heaven is like . . ."), the miraculous healings and all the teachings of Jesus. It is clear that Christ came to proclaim the Kingdom: the Kingdom that was both already within and to yet come.

If the Baptism of Jesus is a clear reference to the importance of our own Baptismal commitment, and if the Wedding Feast at Cana acknowledged the importance of the Sacrament of Marriage, then this Proclamation of the Kingdom calls us to seek the pardon of God in the Sacrament of Reconciliation.

We are all in need of reconciliation. I remember working hard at a Midwestern youth center, which was an extension of our parish for formerly migrant Hispanic families. One day I found myself at wit's end as one of the youth seemed intent upon ruining the activities of the group. We installed a pool table in the basement but this fellow controlled who could use it and dominated the use of it himself. The group painted a house as a service project but this fellow and his buddies found the liquor supply there and the group of them had to be driven home inebriated. When the music group practiced there, the same young man would intimidate the other youth so much that they would not sing out. I had tried lectures and fraternal correction from other youth and it was all to no avail.

Finally this one fine day the young man was acting up again and I just snapped. I had tried everything, or so it seemed. In a fit of anger hardly appropriate for my role as trusted coordinator and adult supervisor of the group, I challenged him to a fight! Can you imagine how much of a breach of the confidence the parents placed in me that move was? I must have been really steaming to have lowered myself to a way of solving problems that the teens already knew all too well. Rather than fight in front of the group, I thought we could "duke it out" away somewhere where I could drive us in my car. Wrong as I was to do it, I stood by my challenge. There would be only one coordinator of this youth group. Maybe because of my collar, or because my frustration made me look fierce, or certainly because God's merciful providence intervened, the young man did not take up the challenge. He simmered down and caused no more trouble. Neither of us had to end up in the hospital that day, but I could see on the faces of the teens that they were confused at the mixed message my challenge represented. The priest challenging someone to a fight just didn't seem right, because it wasn't!

The more I ruminated about it, the more I realized that I had crossed a line as the leader of the group. If the Christian message is about the Kingdom of love, peace, and forgiveness, then I had no business trying to resolve conflicts using the methods of a pugilist. There was no Kingdom teaching in that. But what could I do now that the youths had witnessed my indiscretion?

I decided to make a public confession of the matter. From the pulpit the next Sunday I made the shame-faced announcement that I had transgressed and betrayed the confidence of both the youths and parents by my actions. I humbly asked their pardon and expressed my willingness to step aside as the coordinator of the group if this was what the parishioners wanted. The people of God understood and found forgiveness in their hearts, even if I hadn't. As they left after Mass, many of them admitted that they, too, lost their patience with their teenage sons and daughters at times. Even though this was the case, they were glad I admitted my error and didn't want me to repeat it. But they wanted me to continue to lead the group—in a little more priestly manner. This was both a learning experience and one of reconciliation, which I cherished as the group continued its activities. Many years later, when I returned to the Midwest to officiate at the wedding of the godson of this now grown-up teenager, we were able to laugh at the story and remember old times when the youth socialized and engaged in service projects at the Youth Center.

Forgiveness must be something we can ask for and receive, or be asked for and freely give if we are to call ourselves Christian. It is clear that Jesus Christ did not hesitate to forgive and often told parables and exemplified by his actions this forgiving way of life. The prodigal son and the woman caught in adultery both experienced the forgiveness offered by our loving God through an equally prodigal father or through Jesus himself. Even if we have been offended in some serious way, our response, if it is to be authentic, must be forgiving.

Having forgiven others, we travel more lightly. Having been forgiven, we have more tolerance, understanding, and compassion for the sinner. Let us celebrate true reconciliation with God, others, and ourselves in this beautiful mystery of life.

QUESTIONS FOR REFLECTION

Share with someone a moment of forgiveness you have experienced that brought you closer to Christ.

When have you found it in you to forgive an offense of another? How did you feel about this?

The Transfiguration:
Listen to Him!

Six days later, Jesus took with him Peter and James and his brother John and led them up a high mountain, by themselves. And he was transfigured before them, and his face shone like the sun, and his clothes became dazzling white.

Suddenly there appeared to them Moses and Elijah, talking with him. Then Peter said to Jesus, "Lord, it is good for us to be here; if you wish, I will make three dwellings here, one for you, one for Moses, and one for Elijah."

While he was still speaking, suddenly a bright cloud overshadowed them, and from the cloud a voice said, "This is my Son, the Beloved; with him I am well pleased; listen to him!"

When the disciples heard this, they fell to the ground and were overcome by fear. But Jesus came and touched them, saying, "Get up and do not be afraid." And when they looked up, they saw no one except Jesus himself alone.

Matthew 17:1–8

We are all familiar with this scriptural event. Jesus takes his closest friends, Peter, James, and John, up a high mountain by themselves. He was transfigured before them, his face shining like the sun and his clothes white as light. Moses and Elijah, representing the law and the prophets, appear conversing with him. Peter wishes to construct three tents there on the mountain, perhaps like those used at the festival of booths. It seems that Peter was greatly impressed with seeing the glory of the Lord. It was clear to him then that Jesus was the Son of God. If only Jesus would keep this appearance, then many would come to recognize him. But alas, they finally saw no one else but Jesus, alone.

A bright cloud had cast a shadow over them, and they had heard the voice of the Father repeat the message heard during the Baptism by John, "This is my beloved Son, with whom I am well pleased." Then the voice added: "Listen to him." Jesus is the Son of God; it is clear. Humanly, we would all probably want to take up residence on top of that mountain. But also, we must descend to live our lives in "the valley of tears" here below! In Matthew's account, Jesus then clarifies to the apostles that John the Baptist was the return coming of Elijah, as promised in the Hebrew Testament. He also predicts the suffering of the Son of Man at the hands of those who fail to recognize Elijah.

I'm sure that the memory of this event never faded for Peter, James, and John. It is not every day that one sees the glory of the Lord. In fact, the memory of that day probably strengthened these friends of Jesus to be ultimately faithful to their calling. Once you have seen the glory of the Lord, you are convinced and fortified to do his will. You know he is real and present to you, even when that presence cannot be perceived.

I have seen the glory of the Lord on a few occasions in my life. One was during the summers when I was a seminarian. When I would visit my family as they were living on the shore of a lake in Connecticut, I used to go out and sit on the dock at midnight or so and look on the surface of the lake, where soft moonlight was dancing. This experience seemed always to lead me to prayer praising the Creator of the lake, the moon and its light, myself and all the world. I could stay there for hours in prayer. It wasn't a mountaintop, but I had such a sense of God's enduring love for me as manifested in nature that my faith was strengthened and fortified not only in those moments, but in the later moments of calling those occasions to mind when my prayer had rather dried up. I could not see the glory of the Lord every day, but I could recall those precious moments, and that would always be a consolation to me in prayer.

Do you recall a time when you were at prayer, and you just knew that God was with you and all was right with the world? That is perhaps your mountaintop experience of seeing the glory of the Lord. Now, when the moment is long past, and perhaps you are having a difficult time simply concentrating in prayer, you might recall this witnessing of the glory of the Lord which you once experienced. Bring it all prayerfully back to mind, every detail. Recall the day, the place, the time (as the followers of Jesus in Mark remember it, it was around 4:00 p.m. for them!), and the circumstances. Such a blessed time is worth re-visiting, perhaps when we are feeling most disconnected in our prayer. It is consoling to recall how we have seen the glory of the Lord in our prayer. It can encourage us, as the memory of the Transfiguration of Christ must have encouraged Peter, James, and John!

Another moment in my life when I sensed the presence and glory of God was in my father's final hours on this earth. I had gotten the word that my dad was failing, and that it would not be long before he was called to God. With the company of another Holy Cross priest who offered to come, I drove through a snowstorm for three hours to get to the nursing home where Dad was dying.

It was Alzheimer's disease that claimed my father's life. It is a cruel disease that robs one of memory and a sense of security and identity. But there were three aspects of life that Alzheimer's could not rob my father of: his prayer life, his sense of humor, and his music. My sisters and I (four of my five sisters could be there in person, and the fifth was present by telephone) accompanied my dad in praying the Rosary. Then we shared in some lighter, humorous moments with him, each claiming to be his favorite child. Dad could always laugh at a situation, and this was no exception.

Finally, we started to sing for my dad and he sang along as he could. The nurses must have found us an unusual family, all gathered around my dad's deathbed singing a rousing chorus of "I've been working on the Railroad" followed by "You Are My Sunshine." Then we began singing songs about going home: "Swing Low, Sweet Chariot" and "Soon and Very Soon We Are Going to Meet the King." And we would like to think that as we continued to sing together, he began to hear the music of a much better and bigger heavenly choir, which took over singing the praises of God. It was a holy moment. There was no suffering. Only a going home accompanied by a wonderful Chorus. It was a transfiguration. God revealed His glory.

God is revealed in glory from time to time in our lives. But it takes some training and practice to "listen to him." We are like Martha, busy about many things, but there is only one thing that matters; our relationship with Jesus Christ the Savior and the way that makes us more loving servants of those in need. The word "obedience" means listening. If we would be obedient to God's word, we must shut out the background noise and concentrate on the message. "Speak, Lord, your servant is listening" must be our prayer. Then encouraged and enlightened by our transfiguration experience, we can do whatever he tells us. We will have that confidence that we have heard the word of God and kept it.

QUESTIONS FOR REFLECTION

Try to recall your own mountaintop experience. Cherish the memories and allow them to enhance your prayer in the present moment.

Where and when have you really encountered the living Lord in your prayer? Describe the luminous moment in your own words.

The Institution of the Eucharist: Wash Each Other's Feet

Now before the festival of the Passover, Jesus knew that his hour had come to depart from this world and go to the Father. Having loved his own who were in the world, he loved them to the end. The devil had already put it into the heart of Judas, son of Simon Iscariot, to betray him. And during supper Jesus, knowing that the Father had given all things into his hands, and that he had come from God and was going to God, got up from the table, took off his outer robe, and tied a towel around himself. Then he poured water into a basin and began to wash the disciples' feet and to wipe them with the towel that was tied around him.

After he had washed their feet, had put on his robe, and had returned to the table, he said to them, "Do you know what I have done to you? You call me Teacher and Lord—and you are right, for that is what I am. So if I, your Lord and Teacher, have washed your feet, you also ought to wash one another's feet. For I have set you an example, that you also should do as I have done to you."

John 13:1–4, 12–15

The Mass is the source and summit of our Christian life. The Eucharist is the presence of Jesus Christ in the Mass, so at long last, the Eucharist is now one of the mysteries the Rosary, as suggested by Pope John Paul II in *Rosarium Virginis Mariae*. The Lamb of God found a way to nourish us frequently at the altar, giving us his body and blood.

It is notable that the Holy Father did not choose the words of institution as the first Scripture passage to explain this Mystery. Instead, he chose John's account of the foot-washing, portrayed so vividly in the Holy Thursday liturgy. Jesus removed his cloak, wrapped a towel around his waist, and proceeded to wash the feet of the apostles. When he had finished, he said to them, "Take note of what I have done. You call me Teacher and Lord, and it is right that you do. If I who am Teacher and Lord have washed your feet, then so, too, must you wash each other's feet" (Jn 13:12–14).

As we approach the Eucharist with frequency, this is a good teaching for us to take in: the reason for our closeness to the Eucharist is the service we can render to each other after the Master's example. Our reception of communion is meant to make us more loving and thereby more like Christ, more willing to serve.

Have you ever had your feet washed as a part of a welcoming ceremony? I have, in Dinaspur, Bangladesh, on the occasion of my giving a talk on the Rosary. Young girls came forward with an elaborate and colorful dance. They were holding a washbowl and pitcher. I must have had the same reaction Peter did, because a part of me wanted to protest and say, "You should never wash *my* feet!" It was a public event. It was embarrassing to have my feet washed when others did not. But I knew it was a gesture of warm welcoming for the special guest who was going to speak about the Rosary, including this particular mystery, so I finally consented much as Peter had, saying, "then my hands and my head as well!" If what is being celebrated here is the significance of this new Luminous Mystery, then so be it. What struck me was how receiving is more difficult and humbling than giving! Jesus allowed the woman to wash his feet with her tears and anoint them with perfumed oil. He also allowed the people to welcome him into Jerusalem with palm branches waving and cloaks laid down in his path. The people cried "Hosanna!" though others would soon cry "Crucify him!"

The message of the Eucharist, in the last exhortation of the Mass, is *Ite Misa Est!* This is not simply: "Go, the Mass is ended!" It rather implies: "Go! You are sent, missioned as a missionary to live the mysteries we have just celebrated here. But now go live those same mysteries of thanksgiving and service. Go: live it all out there in the world, which needs to know the love of God through your behavior!" *Ite Misa Est* says a great deal about living the faith we have celebrated in this sacrificial banquet. Having received the very Body and Blood of the Savior, we are commissioned *(Misa)* to go forth and share this Good News with all the world! Each of us, baptized as priest, prophet, and king, must do this.

It can be frustrating at times to try and live out the gospel, to be a member of a Eucharistic, foot-washing people. I do much traveling in my work with Holy Cross Family Ministries. I always dress as a priest when I travel, and that gets me into many conversations. Once while traveling by plane I met a Hispanic gentleman from Central America. He had no luggage with him and seemed sad, probably unable to understand even the instructions of the airline attendants or the pilot when he came on to explain that the aircraft was having computer problems and that we would have to land in Dallas for a time in order to have this repaired. I translated for him what was to happen. He had been explaining to me how sad he was that he was being deported back to his country. As he shared his ordeal, I listened with empathy. After all, as a priest I had learned Spanish to be able to communicate in a compassionate way with God's people, such as this gentleman. I gave him the phone number of an immigration lawyer I knew in California (my sister, Peg, the basketball player who had shortened her name, married, and was raising a family). I gave him an extra pair of socks I had in my luggage because he had no socks. I felt that in some small way I was doing whatever I could to live the gospel in this man's presence. Unfortunately, I really could do nothing to stop the deportation.

We touched down in Dallas and said our good-byes to one another. An attendant in the airport explained in English how we could come forward to get our lunch vouchers from the airline. I translated for the Spanish speaker once again, and we marched together, vouchers in hand, to get our lunch at a restaurant. I knew now why our God had brought us together: so I could guide my lost friend here. We filled our plates and found a table. I sat down, famished, and began eating. He remained standing and blessed himself for grace. Turning red now in my collar, and hoping no one noticed, I stood and joined in the prayer. How embarrassing, not to give thanks to God for this food! The man sat down to eat and first explained that he was not trying to make me feel uncomfortable. "You see, Father," he said in Spanish, "I had to give thanks for this meal. I haven't eaten in three days."

Sometimes the effort to live the Eucharist results in our receiving so much more than what we have to give. Our God has a way of forming the Body of Christ and strengthening it. And God's ways are not our ways!

I often wonder about and pray for the man from Central America. He had no socks, no luggage, no standing in this country, and no mastery of English; and he had had no food for three days. But he had faith, perhaps a greater blessing than any of these. And his spirit of gratitude continues to inspire me, especially as I go to the Eucharistic table. God sends such folks to us to evangelize us, even as we think we are evangelizing them!

QUESTIONS FOR REFLECTION

How does it change your life in a given week to have received the Holy Eucharist on Sunday? Can others see the connection between your reception of the Eucharist and your Christian treatment of them?

Christ came to serve and not to be served. What service to the wider community are you engaged in out of the motivation you get from living the Gospel and receiving Holy Communion?

LIVING THE SORROWFUL

MYSTERIES

The Agony in the Garden: Not as I Will, but as You Will

Then Jesus went with them to a place called Gethsemane; and he said to his disciples, "Sit here while I go over there and pray." He took with him Peter and the two sons of Zebedee and began to be grieved and agitated. Then he said to them, "I am deeply grieved, even to death; remain here, and stay awake with me." And going a little farther, he threw himself on the ground and prayed, "My Father, if it is possible, let this cup pass from me; yet not what I want but what you want."

Matthew 26:36–39

His soul was "deeply grieved, even to death" as he asked his closest friends, Peter, James, and John, to remain and keep watch with him as he prayed at Gethsemane. Of course, those close friends were not as aware as he was of the ordeal he was to undergo, even though Jesus had foretold his demise at the hands of sinners and even his resurrection from the dead. Peter had just promised that he would never deny Jesus, even if he should have to die with him.

Asking his friends to keep watch with him, he advanced and fell prostrate in prayer, saying "My

Father, if it is possible, let this cup pass from me; yet, not as I will, but as you will." Returning to his friends, he found them asleep. This pattern happened three times, like the three times Peter would deny him, and the three times the risen Christ would ask Peter if he loved him and then commission him to feed his sheep. Each time, Jesus' closest friends slept as he went through his agony, praying that the cup might pass without his having to drink it, but conceding that the Father's will must be done.

Suffering is made worse when your closest loved ones are unaware of your sad ordeal and unaffected by it, unable to join you in prayer as friends full of compassion. W. H. Auden, the poet, puts it this way:

> About suffering they were right
> The old masters;
> How it goes on while
> The executioner's horse
> Blithely scratches his behind
> On a tree.

Suffering is made all the worse by our inattentiveness to the suffering of others, even those closest to us. The executioner's horse could not care less about the dramatic scene of execution of which he was a part. Jesus' closest friends slept until awakened with "Get up. Let us go. Look, my betrayer is at hand."

Where have I lived this kind of scene? I remember our family used to vacation at Bantam Lake in Connecticut each year. My sisters and brother and I all enjoyed swimming in the lake, playing cards if it rained, just relaxing in down time during a few lazy summer weeks. One day my sister Susan jumped off the dock and cut her foot on some glass in the lake. I was floating in a tube at the time looking at the clouds. Susan was bleeding, though she wasn't crying, and my mom and some others were tending to her, wrapping her foot in a towel. "Should I go offer a helping hand? Oh, I think they have it covered. There is nothing I could do. I'll stay and continue examining cloud formations," I thought to myself.

Just then I heard my folks calling me with a commanding tone. "We're taking Susan to the hospital, Johnny. Get out of the water and into the car!" "But wait a minute," I protested. "I didn't cut *my* foot. Why should I go to the hospital?" The answer came quickly, "You know that when your father and I are not around, you and your sister Betsy start fighting with each other! Get in the car!"

There was no avoiding it. My past and likely future scuffles with my oldest sister were costing me a dear price, a car ride to the hospital when I wasn't even sick. Susan, her foot wrapped in a towel but still bleeding, was quiet in the back seat along with me. My mother's anxiety was showing itself as she instructed my dad when to speed up or slow down or where to turn. Dad was calmly ignoring these instructions. Mom's little finger, curled around the little vent window cars used to have in those days, was turning white. There was tension in the air.

We finally arrived after our hurried ride over narrow country roads. We all got out of the car and slammed the doors, eager for Susan to get to the doctor so the bleeding foot could be mended. Susan started to panic. Her face turned bright red and she cried, even screamed. She was standing by the car wailing so that she could hardly catch her breath. "Don't cry, Susan!" we were saying. "The doctor's your friend. He'll fix your foot. You've been to the doctor before. Don't be afraid of the doctors!" I tried to help by tugging at her free hand to get her to move toward the emergency room. That's when she caught her breath enough to utter, "My hand's caught in the door!" I still do not recall if it was Susan's helpful little brother who had slammed the door on her hand, but at least the mystery of why Susan was behaving this way was solved. The blackened fingers required the attention of the doctor before the bleeding foot could be stitched.

Suffering is always worse when your loved ones, standing around you, really are unaware of its severity. Ultimately, all suffering is personal. We prefer not to suffer, but for us Christians, we pray that God's will, not ours, be done. We know we cannot get through this life without having to suffer. But we do what we can to avoid it. The challenge is to be more Good Samaritan than sleeping apostle when it comes to accompanying another in his or her suffering. Too often in life our song is "Nobody knows the troubles I've seen. Nobody knows but Jesus."

Jesus did not miss the sufferings of others or ignore them to carry on his own agenda. He was outgoing and compassionately understanding toward the woman at the well, the adulterous woman about to be stoned, the lepers who cried out for healing, the children who wanted to be near him, and the official whose son was dying. Suffering has some value to it, especially if endured because God's will must be done. We may be helpless to avoid it, but we can offer it up for particular purposes. Servant of God Father Peyton used to visit the sick and ask them to offer their sufferings for the success of the Family Rosary rally that was to be held. This gave those who were suffering a reason to endure what came in order that God's will be done.

When have you endured sufferings that others close to you were totally unaware of? I think of the person who has been given a diagnosis of cancer and has not told anyone yet; or perhaps the young girl who is pregnant and unwed and agonizing about how to tell anyone, feeling alone and fearful.

Jesus' agony was terrible, as in his humanity he wanted to avoid suffering if possible but ultimately prayed that God's will be done. No one was able to share that decision with him. It came from his own personal integrity. When we pray this sorrowful mystery, may we think of the sufferings we endure without others being aware enough or able to alleviate them. May we also examine ourselves as to the quality or frequency of our compassionate presence to those who undergo great suffering. "Not as I will, but as You will!"

QUESTIONS FOR REFLECTION

Tell of a time when you underwent suffering and were not consoled by loved ones around you.

Are there moments when your compassionate awareness of the suffering of others is lacking? (For example, I once visited with a woman in the hospital who seemed a bit uncomfortable about something, but I didn't know what. We discussed her illness and prayed together. As I made my exit, I noticed a nurse rushing in to get her off the bedpan!)

The Scourging at the Pillar:
Pilate Took Jesus
and Had Him Scourged

Then Pilate took Jesus and had him flogged.

John 19:1

Most who have seen the movie *The Passion of the Christ* found the scene of the scourging at the pillar to be most gruesome and difficult to watch. As the whipping tore the flesh of the Savior, the brutality of this Roman practice was obvious. If crucifixion was to warn the Jews against any possible uprising against the Roman occupation, then the scourging was intended to weaken the victim and shorten the time he would hang on the cross before asphyxiation. The touching scene in the movie shows Mary taking cloths given to her by Pilate's wife and sopping up the blood of her son with them. Mary is there for the sad scene, and certainly the mockery and mistreatment of the scourgers was a terrible scene for her to witness.

Where do we see Jesus scourged today? I have long thought that it is where there is abuse, especially in the family. That is where the flesh of the incarnate God is torn mercilessly. Jesus had such love for the children and encouraged his followers to become like them, perhaps in their sense of wonder at all the beauty of creation and the many blessings they see in the world; perhaps in their total dependence upon the Father; perhaps in their ability to play and use their imagination while showing total trust in the adults who look after their safety.

But alas, in the real world children are abused, sometimes by their own fathers. There are many forms of abuse: physical, emotional, verbal, sexual; even noise pollution is a kind of abuse. Sometimes the home is besieged by noise from TV, radio, the Internet, video games, people yelling such that no one can do his or her homework because there is no peace. Children brought up in such an environment are certainly deprived. Jesus is scourged again today when children are abused in any of these ways in the family locale, where they should be protected and guided by the adult generation.

What of the sexual abuse of children by priests, you might ask. This, too, is the scourging at the pillar. I make no excuses for priests or religious whose position of trust they betrayed by abusing minors. Such acts are despicable. While any instance of such abuse is too many, I must observe as well that Catholic clergy are not the only folks to have committed such atrocities, even though you might get a different impression from today's newspapers. The majority of instances of pedophilia and, of course, incest take place in the home by relatives of the victims. This is a problem in the whole of our society. If the Church experience of facing this crisis can begin to help those in public schools, hospitals and nursing homes, scouting organizations, counseling situations, various professions, and at home in families deal with the problem in those societal contexts, then all the current attacking and critiquing of the Church—guilty as it is in many cases—will not have been in vain.

Where else have I seen Jesus scourged in our time? One place in particular is the prison system. One of the most difficult roles of the prison chaplain is to inform an inmate of the death of his mother or some other close relative. I remember once bracing myself to be able to pick up the pieces if the prisoner fell apart, knowing he would be informed of a death and given the stark choice of either calling his closest remaining relative now to express his condolences or showing up in chains and with armed escorts in a manner unannounced to attend the wake or funeral in person. This one man was ushered into the office I was using. I said something like: "I am sorry to tell you that your mother died last night." The response came with a shrug of the shoulders: "Yeah. So, you got a smoke on you, Chaplain?" Apparently, his mom was not close to him and never raised him. His grandmother's death would have been much harder for him to take because she had raised him. There are many such examples of Jesus being scourged today. So many imprisoned today were abused when they were children, and this created (or at least contributed to the creation of) a rage within them that moved them swiftly toward incarceration.

Another example was when I officiated at a wake service for the infant child of a homeless woman who was addicted to drugs. When I got to the funeral parlor, the mother was sitting at the back of the room, too ashamed to go forward and peer into the tiny white coffin. Her conscience would not allow her to mix with the few people there. She knew that her own use of drugs was what caused the stillbirth. She had no intention of taking care of her own health or making the sacrifices a mother makes to bring a child to term. What a sorrowful scourging at the pillar!

To look at the reality of the scourging of Jesus at the pillar today is a sorrowful task. It is to look at the reality of evil in our time. Child pornography, for example, is a huge business in our time, and predators on the Internet are dangerous. All children should enjoy a carefree childhood in which they are loved and affirmed and never demeaned or abused. The Evil One is successful among us when selfishness and pleasure-seeking blind us to what we actually are doing.

Let us pray that the seed of God's word will fall on better soil in our time. The corrective the Church hierarchy has undergone these past years was apparently very necessary. Let us pray that it leads to a wider corrective for the rest of our society, calling us all to honesty and purity of heart and consciousness of the respect we owe every living person. Jesus did not deserve to be scourged for his message of love and reconciliation. Neither does any brother or sister merit abuse that treats them as sex objects or people with no rights. God forgive us for our scourging of the Savior.

QUESTIONS FOR REFLECTION

Have you been abused in any of the ways described in this chapter? How have you dealt with this experience?

It is easy for us to think and say that we would never have given our consent to the flogging of Jesus. Yet, in our time, are there situations of real abuse that we have condoned by our silence, afraid to cause trouble?

The Crowning with Thorns:
Hail, King of the Jews!

And the soldiers wove a crown of thorns and put it
on his head, and they dressed him in a purple robe.
They kept coming up to him, saying, "Hail, King of
the Jews!" and striking him on the face.

John 19:2–3

The passion stories were the first of the many stories about Jesus to circulate by word of mouth when the
early Church was in its infancy. People were amazed at
the extent of the cruelty shown against Jesus. He had
been recognized as coming in the name of the Lord as
a healer, a teacher, and a prophet among the people, so
many having benefited from his manner and his message. He had gained many enemies as he condemned
the self-serving practices, the narrow interpretation of
the law, and the priority of place and honor afforded
the Scribes and Pharisees. The Sanhedrin was highly
offended to see the sign go up above his head on the
cross: "Jesus, the Nazarene, King of the Jews." While
Pilate found no guilt in him, the people threatened to
cause a riot, which would draw the attention of the
Roman authorities on the whole of Israel and on Pilate's

incompetence. And so one man was to suffer and die for the sake of the whole people (Jn 18:14).

What is meant by the giving of a crown of thorns to Jesus? A crown, of course, would be a symbol of authority and leadership. But that it would also be made of a substance causing severe pain and wounds to the head turns this gift into a mockery. Jesus was further given a purple cloak and a reed as a staff. He was buffeted and spat upon by his mocking "subjects." Throughout all this he said nothing. He was blindfolded, and then people knelt before him and slapped him, telling him to divine who it was who slapped him. The crown of thorns was a gruesome form of torture. It was a mocking of the Kingdom of God, which Jesus had presented in his parables, beatitudes, and teachings. In other words, this third sorrowful mystery of the Rosary is the mocking of the third Luminous Mystery, the Proclamation of the Kingdom. His Kingdom was not of this world. Those who scoffed at him recognized him only as a mock king.

Where does this kind of mockery of the Kingdom take place in our world and time? Take a look at how children and young people interact. If one little child lisps or has any deficiency or disability, the others are likely to mock her for it. Children like to enjoy life, and unfortunately one of the ways adults model for them how to enjoy life is at the expense of a neighbor or family member who is somehow different. So young ones learn to imitate the one who suffers from a speech impediment in order to mock him. "Tweens" and teens can get into bullying, a practice that can have such a brutal effect on someone trying to "fit in" to a group of young people that it could (and sometimes does) lead even to suicide.

Adults are not free of the practice of bullying and mockery. Let's say your local church, or even a small club you belong to, has just elected someone (given him or her a crown). It turns out to be a candidate other than the one you may have preferred. (Your candidate may even have been yourself!) So as the crown is being offered, you assure yourself that the crown will be one of thorns. "Just let this new royal leader try to get anything done for this group," you think to yourself. "I will ensure that my friends do not cooperate with such projects, since I would have made a better leader!" The royal leader is given a crown, all right: a painful crown of thorns as a result of others dragging their feet and holding back their real endorsement of leadership by their non-participation. Presidents of countries are sometimes elected this way (given a crown) and then criticized at their decisions and moves as leaders (given thorns in their crown).

Religious communities can end up treating their leadership in this way. New leadership in a contentious election can discover they have no endorsement for their programs. Ministry groups in a parish can behave in the same fashion. "Oh, I forgot the date of the meeting," or "It wasn't clear that you expected me to do that task." Damning with faint praise, we can make quite an entertainment out of non-cooperation and non-compliance as we mock the "kingdoms" led by others. Our own resentfulness for not being elected or getting our way or our poor self-esteem can be our motive, leading us to interpret the success of others as somehow detracting from our own success.

Groups of insecure human beings can often behave as crabs in a bucket. As soon as one crab climbs up the wall of the bucket, making possible an escape from captivity, the other jealous crabs use their pincers to drag it down to the confusion shared by all in the bucket. Infighting and jealous maneuvers can make the success of a chosen leader an experience of a painful crown of thorns.

The apostles bickered with each other about who was the greatest among them. That's when Jesus invited them to be more like children: innocent, trusting, untainted by self-promotion and self-aggrandizement. There is something rather deep in our human condition that urges us to place ourselves somewhere above others. We want to be the greatest, to have the widest impact, to be the most impressive. To this Jesus says, "If you wish to be the greatest of all, then serve all the rest." We are not to show our authority by lording it over one another. Rather, we are to seek the good of the other. May our loving God, who shared with us the inspiring life of his only begotten Son, help us to humble ourselves and seek the common good of all. Give your strength to those who wear the crowns of authority among us. May we place no thorns in those crowns!

QUESTIONS FOR REFLECTION

Tell of a time you have experienced a crown of thorns while trying to give leadership to folks who resisted.

In what ways have you ever inflicted a crown of thorns on others: the president of a group, your pastor, your teacher, your boss, your mentor?

The Carrying of the Cross: So They Took Jesus, and Carrying the Cross by Himself ...

> Then Pilate handed Jesus over to them to be crucified. So they took him; and carrying the cross by himself, he went out to what is called The Place of the Skull, which in Hebrew is called Golgotha.
>
> John 19:16–17

Jesus carried his own cross, at least according to the author of John's gospel, and in doing so he was an example for all of us. We too must bear the cross, or perhaps many crosses, at different times in our lives. Rarely would a person's cross be as severe as the cross of Jesus, given how terrible this form of tortuous, ignominious death was, and how innocent the victim. But innocents do suffer in our time; the innocent victims of war and those who deal with painful, fatal illness have heavy crosses to bear. So, too, do refugees and those who die of starvation in a world of plenty.

Jesus says, "Do not weep for me." But his ordeal was totally humiliating and defeating, according to human judgment. A crucifixion in Roman times was meant to serve as a warning to anyone who would dare to think of leading an uprising. And remember, people had their hopes that this Jesus would be such a leader. They were sorely disappointed and must have found his bearing a cross through the streets of Jerusalem to indicate a complete abandonment by God.

The mystery of suffering has always plagued humanity. How do we explain the fact that a just man like Job would lose everything? How could God allow that? The same must have been asked concerning Jesus: how could God allow that Christ would suffer so? Of course we know that Christ died for our sins, but we also know that carrying the cross of suffering can wear anyone down and even make us resentful, if not despairing.

Yet Jesus bore his cross himself. And following Christ to Calvary, we see the meaning of salvific suffering. We believe that offering up suffering for specific intentions can give that suffering greater meaning. Servant of God Patrick Peyton, C.S.C., used to ask people in the hospital or in nursing homes to offer up their suffering for the success of his Family Rosary Crusade, a campaign to encourage families to pray the Rosary together. Jesus saw what he underwent as having meaning, but humanly it must have drained him completely to have to carry the instrument of his torture and death to Calvary. Where did he get the strength and the grace to do it? From his Father in heaven, whose will he had committed himself to fulfill.

When I worked among the Mexican American community in South Bend, Indiana, I noticed a man who came to the parish only once a year, on Good Friday.

He happened to be a man with one arm who worked very hard in the local day-care center for Hispanic children. He would come up for the kissing of the cross, and always kiss the left arm of Jesus, because that was the arm he lived without. I only noticed this after a few years, as I held the cross. This man always had to kiss that left arm, and that was his participation in the cross of Christ: not the kissing of the crucifix, but his living and working without that arm. I found this man's faith to be inspirational. What a concrete way to recommit oneself to carrying the cross after the example of Christ. What a beautiful way to conform one's life to Christ.

How well do we understand and accept the crosses we have to bear? Do we allow our faith to inform that terrible experience and bless it somehow? After all, if Jesus Christ himself had to undergo such suffering and bear his cross, then why should we not do the same? No one promised us that life would be without suffering. But we were given the example of Jesus undergoing suffering for us and being obedient to the Father's will.

A personal experience of carrying the cross for me has been the death of my brother. He died at age twenty-three and was survived by his wife and two-year-old child. At the time, I was five years ordained. I presided at the Mass of Resurrection for my brother and tried to console family members and deal with my own grief as well as possible, but the loss of my only brother had a very heavy effect upon me.

I had grown up praying the Rosary, whether alone or with the family, but in the seminary I had put it aside, as many did after Vatican II. My ministry with the Mexican American community called for the Rosary, and I prayed it with them for their sake, but in truth, it was not an important part of my personal devotional life.

When I returned to the Midwest from Connecticut where my brother had died, I found myself all but paralyzed by his death. I would go to my office at the youth center each day and accomplish nothing. I was mourning and did not know how to carry this cross. One man from the Mexican community said to me: "Have a novena, Father, in your home. We'll come and pray with you." I knew this custom of praying a novena of Rosaries for a deceased loved one in the home, and I had accompanied many families in their novenas after deaths. I protested, "You did not even know my brother." He answered, "We know you and what you are undergoing right now. Let us accompany you." So I put a picture on a table in the living room, and each night people came to pray the Rosary with me. Those who came were those whom I had accompanied in their novena of Rosaries for loved ones they had lost. I was impressed with that, and I began to realize that ministry is mutual. This experience brought me back to life. It did not make me "get over" my brother's death. I think what we learn to do with a tragic death is just to live with it, knowing that God gives us the necessary grace and friends to share the burden, and a powerful prayer called the Rosary, on which to pray the sorrowful mysteries with new meaning. I've been praying the Rosary daily with renewed enthusiasm ever since.

QUESTIONS FOR REFLECTION

Name a cross that you are bearing now. Describe it to a friend, and ask the Lord's help with it.

Can you remember a Simon of Cyrene who helped you carry your cross? Tell the story.

Has the experience of suffering ever served to strengthen you and make you more compassionate? Explain.

The Crucifixion:
Into Your Hands
I Commend My Spirit

It was now about noon, and darkness came over the whole land until three in the afternoon, while the sun's light failed; and the curtain of the temple was torn in two. Then Jesus, crying with a loud voice, said, "Father, into your hands I commend my spirit." Having said this, he breathed his last.

Luke 23:44–46

As Jesus took upon himself our sins at the moment of his "Baptism of repentance" at the hands of John, so here on the cross he offered his whole life, taking upon himself all our sin. "The one who knew no sin was made sin for our sake," says Paul. This ultimate sacrifice of his life for us was the sure sign of his infinite love. "There is no greater love than this: to lay down one's life for a friend."

Most of us likely hope and pray for a death that is not painful. Jesus prayed for the same, we could conclude, from the scene of his agony in the garden of Gethsemane. At great cost to himself, he then accepted to do his Father's will. On the cross he expressed his feeling of abandonment, his trust that his Father would receive him, his thirst, his forgiveness of the repentant thief, and his forgiveness of his tormentors. And before he was to utter his final words before death, "It is finished," he presented his mother to John and John to his mother in words that conveyed how Mary would be the Mother of the Church.

This is a scene that would cause great despair for those of little faith. The whole mission of Jesus of Nazareth appeared to have been in vain. Only some of the women followers and John stayed with him until the end. The atmosphere was one of cruel mockery: "If he is the Messiah, let him come down from the cross and save himself," the people said. All hope appeared to be gone, and even those who had believed were overcome with disappointment and grief. "But we were hoping that he would be the one to redeem Israel" (Lk 24:21b).

The moment of death can be that way: a sacred moment, but a moment of horrible finality. There are those who die in circumstances like those of the thief crucified at Jesus' side, who was so embittered that he cursed everyone. Sometimes in the parish I would be called upon to celebrate the funeral of someone who picked up another drink after working for years on his or her own recovery from alcoholism, one day at a time. The sickness is so dangerous. Even if one has refused drink for years, if one gives in, the disease picks up where it left off and can leave the person unconscious, in a coma, or dead. How sad to recognize those moments of death, when human weakness and the evil of addiction win out.

However, natural death is not something to be feared. It is a part of life. In fact, no life on this earth is complete without going through death, that last portal through which we bring nothing but our character and our good deeds. I remember once as I was pastoring at a parish in Bedford-Stuyvesant, Brooklyn, how a parishioner from Belize came to me one Friday, asking that I go to a hospital in Manhattan where her brother, who had come to visit, was dying. "He has no parish here, Father, but he wants to see a priest. Please visit him for me and bring him the sacraments!" I explained that my commitments for the weekend were such that I could not get away until 9:00 p.m. on Sunday evening. She accepted that and said she would send a message about when I could come.

I must admit to feeling a bit guilty as all the activities of that weekend played themselves out. I would think of the man on his deathbed awaiting the arrival of a busy priest. I had no assurance that he would live until Sunday evening, but I could not suspend my obligations to be at his side until late on Sunday. I prayed for him as I rode the subway to Manhattan and walked down the hall of the quiet hospital. It was now about 10:00 p.m.

When I got to the room, the man sat up in bed as soon as he saw that I was a priest. I gave him the Sacrament for the Sick and Viaticum, communion for the dying. He was very grateful and at ease, though he was unable to speak. I started to talk to the family, who told me that this man had the custom of praying his Rosary daily. They began telling me about his family back in Belize and of their gratitude that I had come, since the sacraments meant so much to him. As we talked, we looked over to the bed to discover that the man had quietly died. He had left us. "He was waiting for you, Father," the family said. What a beautiful death! He had prayed so many times about the hour of his death! Now it had arrived, and God and Mary were present to him. I was convinced that had I arrived on Friday to anoint him, the man would have died then. It was all very moving, and we all prayed for his soul and in gratitude for his life and faith, which so impressed us all.

This man was prepared to die. His family attested that he was not afraid, but he did want to receive his Lord one more time in Holy Communion. His peaceful death was a tribute to a man of faith.

Common wisdom tells us there are two things in life we can depend upon: death and taxes! Contemplating the death of Christ upon the cross, we cannot help but think of our own deaths. Will we have faith then? Will we be responsive to God's grace? Will there be others to comfort and console us? Will we die at peace with all humanity, having expressed our love to all who really matter to us? God grant all these things. "When we eat this bread and drink this cup, we proclaim your death, Lord Jesus; until you come in glory!"

QUESTIONS FOR REFLECTION

....

Have you experienced a death of a loved one in faith and in peace? Describe this experience.

How have you had to die to yourself in the course of your life?

How do you cope with having had to let go of those you love who have left us in death?

LIVING THE GLORIOUS

MYSTERIES

The Resurrection:
Why Do You Seek
the Living among the Dead?

> The women were terrified and bowed their faces to
> the ground, but the men said to them, "Why do you
> look for the living among the dead? He is not here,
> but has risen."

Luke 24:5

The women went to the tomb to anoint the body of
Jesus. It was early, before dawn. They were wondering
who would roll away the stone for them. When they
got there, the stone had already been rolled away. They
went in, and a young man dressed in white sat by the
empty tomb. He asked, "Why do you seek the living one
among the dead? He is not here, but he has been raised."

Jesus had predicted such a thing, but apparently it
had seemed too preposterous to really believe, this business of rising again after three days! If there is one reality we can observe in this world, it is that when you are
dead, you are dead! There is no living after the life we
lead; at least that is what we see with our eyes and experience when loved ones die.

Or is it? Have you ever known someone who has lived with alcoholism or some other addiction? Such people seem practically dead, and there are many such unfortunates. But some of them have found their way into twelve-step programs and are now living their lives one day at a time, knowing they are still addicted but not making the same poor choices as before. We could easily say of them something similar to what the father of the prodigal son said about his own child: "We had to throw a party; your brother was dead and has come back to life!" If you know someone who is faithful to recovery and is living a much more sane and disciplined life, then you, too, know someone who has "risen from the dead!"

Those who fight off cancer and find themselves in remission after months, or even years, of exhausting treatments often feel like they have risen from the dead, as do prisoners who have committed crimes and have paid the price by serving time. The one who goes through the nightmare of prison and is still able to draw closer to Jesus, leaving with no regrets and thanking God for freedom, is very much like someone "risen from the dead."

For some time, I have served as a chaplain to a prison in upstate New York. Working there, I once met a joyful man who played music for our Masses. He would often say to me, "I'll see you one day on the outside, Father!" I must confess that, while I would go along with his words for the sake of friendship, I had no real expectation of ever seeing him on the "outside," a free man reunited with his family. No, these particular prisoners were "hard core." They had done some terrible things, and the expectation was rather that they would find their way back to the correctional institution once the $40 given them by the prison for their return to New York City ran out. This could (and often did) happen very quickly, whether a prisoner had the intention of staying free for good or not.

Years later, I was arranging the altar after Mass one Sunday, and a whole family appeared at the doorway of the church. I motioned them to come forward: a father, mother, and four children. The guitar the man carried gave him away. He was that same musician who had always said he would look me up "on the outside." They were all grinning ear to ear. He testified that his faith had grown while he was in prison, and that his family had suffered without him, missing him for many years. The man was deeply grateful to his family for not giving up on him. He was someone "risen from the dead" in my book. He was even playing music for Sunday Mass in a neighborhood nearby. He and his family knew he would never return to prison.

Another prison story comes to mind. I had been preparing a couple for marriage in the Church. They already had children and were married civilly, but now he was in jail, she was at home raising the children, and they decided to marry in the Church while he was still incarcerated. We had several preparation sessions on prisoner visiting days. Preparations for the wedding day were made—this mostly involved paperwork—and the day finally came.

The wedding was to take place in the front offices of the prison. Having to take on the burden of doubling for a place of worship and celebration, the offices looked especially drab that day. Two secretaries none of us knew acted as the witnesses. The bride appeared, crying in frustration. She had wanted to put some dignity into the meager ceremony. Knowing that the office was bleak and undesirable as a location for her wedding, she had brought her husband a new necktie. Unfortunately, the presence of a necktie was a problem in a maximum security prison. She became infuriated when the officials observed that her husband might hang himself with it! "On his wedding day?!" she protested. After much discussion and many tears, the watch commander finally allowed the tie for the ceremony alone. (He became my hero after that concession.)

In came the groom, dressed in prison green. His hands were cuffed. He did not look happy to see his wife crying. He was escorted by a guard, who had to check the memo to be sure this necktie was allowed. He handed the tie to the inmate, who looked sorrowfully to me. I was dressed in my vestments for the ceremony. It became clear that this man did not know how to tie a tie. I put the tie around my own neck (this being the only way I could get a good knot in the tie), and before the bride could start crying again, I started to laugh at how ridiculous this all looked: a handcuffed prisoner marrying the woman of his dreams in a dreary office with a guard on duty; unknown secretaries as witnesses; and a vested priest tying a tie around his own neck. A bizarre scene indeed! But the sacrament took, and the two have some unusual stories to tell of their wedding. Free of the red tape and the correctional institution, these two qualify as having "risen from the dead!"

Of course, these are simply human experiences—events that give us a kind of hint about the resurrection from the dead. Jesus' resurrection tops them all. But the point here is that if we have experienced some sorrowful mysteries in life, we have also experienced some form of resurrection glory, albeit limited.

We can all look forward to our own resurrection of the body on the last day. Then our experiences of mini-resurrection will be validated, and we will be in the presence of our Creator, having been brought into new life. Death is truly a new beginning. The cross always finds a way to bring hope. So he is risen. He is not here. Why seek the living one among the dead?

QUESTIONS FOR REFLECTION

Have you ever come across someone who has "risen from the dead"? Tell the story.

Have you ever been able to "give new life" to a group or to a depressed or grieving individual? How did you do it? Or, how did God do it through you?

The Ascension:
Make Disciples of All Nations

> Go, therefore, and make disciples of all nations,
> baptizing them in the name of the Father and of the
> Son and of the Holy Spirit . . .
>
> Matthew 28:19

The ascension of Jesus Christ is recounted twice
by Luke: once in his gospel and once in the Acts of the
Apostles. The ascension is the turning point upon which
the gospel ends and the accounts of Acts begin. It is the
final movement of the Paschal Mystery. Jesus has suffered, died, been buried, and has risen from the dead
on the third day. Now he returns to his Father, having
completed his work. He blesses his followers and leaves
them with a commission, recorded in Matthew 28: they
are to go forth and teach all nations, baptizing them in
the name of the Father and of the Son and of the Holy
Spirit.

Jesus' life, death, and resurrection have been directed toward the moment when he would leave his followers to carry on the mission. They have heard all they
needed to hear. They have witnessed miraculous events.
They have been both rebuked and encouraged by the

one who had a special way of treating people in need. Now the challenge is given: can they love like him, forgive like him, lead like him?

The answer is surely negative, and they know it. Who will they entrust with the leadership of the group? Peter, who denied his Lord three times? James and John, whose mother wanted places of special honor in the Kingdom for her sons? Thomas, who doubted the resurrection until he could touch Jesus' wounds? Matthew, who everyone knew was involved in a cheating profession as tax collector?

As the apostles looked around after the ascension of Christ, they realized each other's weaknesses. The men in white told them to stop looking up into the sky. Jesus would return on the last day. They were now supposed to get to work, waiting until Pentecost before leaving the city.

Those men in white could have been angels, or they could have been neophytes, newly baptized Christians, dressed in white and charging the Church to be faithful to their own baptismal commitment. Maybe Luke wrote them into the story because the Church was growing at this early time, and adults were entering into and renewing it by their commitment. Isn't it true today that newly baptized adult converts often call us to be more authentic in the way we live our faith?

The ascension happens whenever a charismatic leader or founder—the one we all depend upon—leaves, and we are all left standing there. We look up into the sky with the apostles and wonder aloud, "Now what? Who will lead us? How are we to carry on? Who of us has the vision or ability that he or she had?" Who indeed?! Not one of the apostles had all of Jesus' gifts. But the young people, like the one in the tomb dressed in white, the ones whose presence encourages us that there are new followers who reinforce our number, tell us simply to stop looking up and start looking around to get to work ourselves. "You give them something to eat!" Jesus had said at the multiplication of the loaves. We are it! We're all that are left, no more, no less—just as we are! And we must honor Jesus' memory by continuing his mission.

It is strange that, when the time comes to claim authority, we can be so reticent and fearful. Much of our early lives is spent in eager anticipation of being in charge—and in intense preparation for it. Then it comes—this thing called responsibility. We look around and see that we're it! Our generation is now in charge. Little did we know that folks as incompetent as us would be the ones who rushed headlong into marriage and raising a family. Who would have thought that bosses don't know everything; that teachers are always learners; that faith, like self-confidence, comes and goes as the tide? Thank God for grace and guardian angels. Thank God that we cannot foresee all the challenges that will present themselves at once. Thank God that life prepares us more than we realize to be strong, to make good decisions, to persevere in adversity, to lead after the one who has led us: Jesus the Christ, risen and ascended into heaven.

My mom brought seven children into the world and always emphasized the importance of the faith. My sister Peg has five children of her own and often finds herself speaking the words of her mother to her children: "Be careful!" "Watch out!" "Don't run!" "Take your time!" "A galloping horse wouldn't stop to look at you." (Peg's hardly ever seen a galloping horse.) "Like it or lump it!" She is just as adamant about the faith dimension of life. My mom and her convictions live on in another generation. (When my mother died, the one member of the family who was not able to be present at the moment of death was Peg. She was living far away and expecting another child. But my mom, always the forceful leader, found a way to include her in the time of her parting; she died on Peg's birthday.)

The ministry I am engaged in now is another good example of having to carry on somehow after the charismatic leader is gone. Servant of God Father Patrick Peyton, C.S.C., was a great figure in American Church history. Convinced that he had been cured of tuberculosis when he was a seminarian, he devoted himself to doing Mary's work by promoting the family Rosary. He used radio, TV, film, and rallies that sometimes involved hundreds of thousands of people to spread his message, as well as his own ability to inspire by the sincerity of his faith and his speech.

When Father Peyton died in 1992, there simply did not exist another Patrick Peyton to replace him. The challenge, then, was to continue the work with the less talented folks we did have (people like myself!). I needed lots of help, and I got it from the Holy Cross Congregations. Together, we have institutionalized Father Peyton's work in the absence of his more charismatic leadership.

We do what we can, and although we sometimes wish that Father Peyton could return to give us clearer direction, we know that is not going to happen. All we can do is use the different talents and personalities we have to continue the work, and we count on Our Lady's intercession and God's good grace to do the rest. We needed to stop looking up at the sky and get to work, helping each other to preserve a ministry that greatly helps families around the world. It was ministry worth doing (it still is), so God found a way, through others who did not have the same gifts, to encourage us again to go forth and make disciples of all nations. We miss our founder, but we carry on. And we know we are not alone. Jesus Christ, in ascending to the Father, left his followers in a similar situation.

QUESTIONS FOR REFLECTION

When have you faced the challenge of carrying on after the leader was no longer there?

Do you pray for the ability to accept responsibility when and as it comes? How has God been responding?

*Does the Rosary help you to conform your life to
Christ even after the death or departure of a loved
one or mentor? Explain.*

Pentecost:
Tongues as of Fire

When the day of Pentecost had come, they were all together in one place. And suddenly from heaven there came a sound like the rush of a violent wind, and it filled the entire house where they were sitting. Divided tongues, as of fire, appeared among them, and a tongue rested on each of them. All of them were filled with the Holy Spirit and began to speak in other languages as the Spirit gave them ability.

Now there were devout Jews from every nation under heaven living in Jerusalem. And at this sound the crowd gathered and was bewildered because each one heard them speaking in the native language of each. Amazed and astonished, they asked, "Are not all these who are speaking Galileans? And how is it that we hear, each of us, in our own native language? Parthians, Medes, Elamites, and residents of Mesopotamia, Judea and Cappadocia, Pontus and Asia, Phrygia and Pamphylia, Egypt and the parts of Libya belonging to Cyrene, and visitors from Rome, both Jews and proselytes, Cretans and Arabs—in our own languages we hear them speaking about God's deeds of power." All were amazed and perplexed, saying to one another, "What does this mean?"

Acts 2:1–12

God poured out a portion of the Spirit upon the young Christian community that fateful day in Jerusalem. At this time, "Pentecost" was already an established feast. The Jewish custom was for the whole family to stay up the whole night long to celebrate the feast of Shavuot, a harvest festival that also commemorated the presentation of the ten commandments by Moses fifty days after the Exodus from Egypt. This was the context in which this first Christian community was gathered in Jerusalem. They were thanking God for the commandments and awaiting at the same time God's command as to what they were to do next. In one gospel they are told to wait in Jerusalem until the promised Holy Spirit would come.

And suddenly there came the noise like a strong, driving wind. The tongues of fire came, and they were all filled with the Holy Spirit and began to speak in different tongues. These tongues were different languages, all understood by a variety of different people from different lands. But they could also represent the different way of speaking of those who know God and whose entire manner of treating others is changed once the Holy Spirit takes over.

Have you ever had the experience comforting a friend after he or she lost a beloved family member, someone who died an untimely death? Did you wonder what to say because the death was tragic or untimely and you knew your friend was devastated? Perhaps you prayed about what to say. "I'm sorry for your loss" never seems quite right. Yet, when you arrived and met your friend, all of a sudden you began to speak some very consoling words, words that seemed to calm and encourage. The friend was grateful for your presence and your words of condolence, but you were left wondering, "Where did all those words come from?"

Such words are from the Holy Spirit, who can take over and give us the words when there are in fact no words to say. The Rosary works this way as well when used at a wake service. The Holy Spirit can take over and calm everyone as they pray in the rhythm of human life.

The Holy Spirit is involved in the Eucharistic liturgy as well. At one point, the priest extends his hands over the gifts of bread and wine at the Offertory and calls down the Spirit's presence and power to change these gifts into the body and blood of the Lord. The same gesture is used at Confirmation, Ordination, and the Sacrament for the Sick. The Holy Spirit is called down upon the one to be confirmed or healed. There is a recognition in this of the power of God to work through human instruments. "Come, Holy Spirit" is as good a prayer as any, especially when there is a crisis or a matter that leaves us at a loss for words.

One experience involving the Holy Spirit that I will never forget is that of preaching at an African American Catholic parish. Some parishes in the tradition of the African -American community expect their priests to come prepared to preach for close to one hour. I have had the experience of entering into such a Sunday project at a Eucharistic liturgy that lasted three hours from start to finish.

Preaching to certain African Americans can be a dialogical proposition. They expect to give you immediate feedback about how you are doing. They will either speak out with "Amen!" or "Tell it now!" or "Say it like it is, Brother!" or they will be silent and perfectly still, thereby expressing a lack of interest in where the homily is going. It's usually quite easy to perceive how the congregation is feeling about the homily and the preacher, judging by just the number and intensity of the "Amen" outbursts.

I actually prefer this kind of dialogue during a homily, as opposed to preaching to a very wooden New England gathering, which will have the same blank expression when you are "bombing out" as when you are converting hearts. No news is not good news when preaching to an African American congregation, and conversely, you'll be told when you are really hitting the mark while preaching.

This communal way of coming up with a homily is truly the effect of the Spirit working through many people. Most who listen to a homily are looking for inspiration to do the right thing. They want to see the gospel applied in concrete ways to their own daily living experience. They are not looking for theological musings, though they want what is said to be in accordance with good theology. They want to be able to evaluate how well or poorly they are living out the particular gospel of the day. They want to be touched by the Word of God and by the Spirit. They want to be encouraged in their journey of faith!

I have found myself, on occasion, starting out in one direction while giving a homily, but then realizing there is very little response coming from the congregation. So I begin to add a few side comments. One of them gets an enthusiastic response, and my homily takes a turn in that direction. Before I know it, I'm preaching on an aspect of the text I had not prepared to preach on. The people have urged me to go there. They have "taken over" the homily and implored the Holy Spirit to "take over" my preaching. They are very well aware of what they have done, and so am I. They want the fire of the Holy Spirit to be manifest in them, and if I would serve them well, I had better go along and start speaking another language!

So whenever we find ourselves speaking words we had not prepared ourselves to say, words that truly console and encourage others, or even challenge others in constructive ways, we know that we are experiencing a kind of Pentecost. The Holy Spirit is probably much closer to us in this situation than we think! In like fashion, when we experience the charity, joy, peace, patience, kindness, generosity, faithfulness, gentleness, and self-control that St. Paul reminds us are fruits of the Holy Spirit (Gal 5:22–23), then we know we are under the influence of the Advocate promised us by the Son of God. We may not even be able to recognize ourselves when we are under this influence, for we will have time for others; if we have to correct others, we will do so gently; we will no longer be conceited, provoking others, or envious of them. A whole new spirit will surround us, and it will be of God! What a difference it would make if we were to walk under God's influence always! We ourselves might even be surprised with the ways God would work through us.

I am reminded of a married couple in a Hispanic community where I once worked. The woman, someone who loved God deeply, always seemed ready with a homily about God's love, and she would preach it often. The truth was, however, many found her off-putting and even tended to avoid her preaching, so it did not convert many. After a while, her husband took to balancing his wife's preaching with jokes—sometimes off-color ones! They were quite a pair, and if their words were not particularly of the Holy Spirit, their actions were!

They were generous to anyone new to the community who was in need of friendship or help in raising their children, or even food or housing. They owned several houses in the town and lent them out, rent-free if necessary, to folks just getting started. This endeared them to everyone, even those with no interest in their homilies or their jokes. When it came down to it, this was a Christian couple whose corporal works of mercy were definitely inspired by the Holy Spirit. The tongues of fire were like slow-burning pilot lights for each of them, which could be fanned into Christ-like generosity and love at any given time!

Questions for Reflection

....

Tell of a time when the Holy Spirit supplied the words, since you did not know what to say.

Has the Spirit ever surprised you with gifts of peace, gentleness, and self-control when others were panicking? Explain.

Has the Spirit ever put fiery words into your mouth in defense of the under-privileged or oppressed? Explain.

The Assumption:
Pray for Us Sinners

I will put enmity between you and the woman, and between your offspring and hers; he will strike at your head while you strike at his heel.

Genesis 3:15

Catholics believe that Mary was assumed into heaven, body and soul. This dogma was defined only in 1950, but it was understood in the tradition of the Church for many centuries. Mary is the Mother of the Savior, Jesus Christ. She was given to all of us in the Church at the foot of the cross: "Son, behold your Mother." John represented all of us that fateful day. Mary was also shown to be the Mother of the Church on another fateful day, when the same Spirit who had overshadowed her at the Annunciation overshadowed the apostles, making of those fearful men evangelizers and courageous witnesses to the gospel. They spoke in many languages and converted three thousand that day. According to tradition, almost all of them would die for the gospel.

What is the significance of that Assumption? It is a prefiguring of our own bodily resurrection. The "resurrection of the body" is of one of the elements of our creed. We believe that, like Mary, we, too, will rise from the dead, body and soul. We proclaim this belief every Sunday. While we do not know much about the condition of our resurrected bodies, we presume them to be like that of the resurrected Christ.

Everything about Mary is related to Christ. She serves as the first among the Saints in the great heavenly communion, whose role it is to pray and intercede for the rest of us here on earth. Her intercession is perhaps so powerful because she is in the presence of her Son. And she prays for all of her other sons and daughters to be in Christ's presence one day as well.

As the Mother of Christ, the Spouse of the Holy Spirit, and the Icon of the Church, Mary lives a story that is the story of the Church. We are Mary's sons and daughters, as are all other Christians. As she was a model of prayer and assent to the will of God in her life on earth, Mary, now assumed into heaven, prays for us still. Any mother is concerned for the welfare of her children, so we can expect that our destiny is a subject of Mary's prayer, and we look forward to the day of the final coming of Christ, when we, too, will be taken to our Creator.

Mary is the Mother essential to the births of both Jesus and the Church. What if she had refused to become that Mother or simply changed her mind? What would we do without the precious gifts of Jesus and the Church? Our lives would certainly be devoid of hope.

In our time, many would-be mothers, often prompted by would-be fathers and even their own parents, change their minds about the desirability of children already on the way. They decide to abort a child before birth and thereby thwart whatever God's plan would be for a life full of potential and filled with the Holy Spirit. Sometimes this is done because the mother fears the harsh judgment of others or worries that a new life will be unaffordable. The unfortunate "would-be mothers" become "would-not-be mothers," refusing to pass on the God-given gift of life. Sometimes the motive is one of mere inconvenience. Instead of nourishing a new generation by passing on the values—especially those of faith—she has received, each "would-not-be mother" stifles the human life within her and makes of her womb a tomb.

The death of a life *in utero,* when it happens spontaneously, can be a terrible trial and burden for those who hope for a safe birth and a healthy child. Their grief can be difficult to console; their disappointment heavy and understandable. But the purposeful ending of a life before birth, in the name of a person's control over her body or in the name of freedom of choice, cries out to heaven. This is a slaughter of innocents. It is an affront to the God of life, whose Son, born by a mother's fiat, gave his life that we might have eternal life. Such a person's remorse can be unbearable; an agonizing, lifelong, haunting "what if . . . ?"

At the moment of her Assumption, Mary, the Mother through whose willing supportive and nourishing presence both Jesus and the Church were born, takes leave of the nascent Church. The Church will certainly miss her. No one knew Christ as well as his Mother did, so the early church must have depended upon her. But her spirit, like the Holy Spirit whom she knows so intimately, remains with the Church, magnifying the presence of the Lord, proclaiming how God raises up the lowly and lets the rich go away empty.

We must be as mothers to those who are distraught over past serious sins of abortion. The sin is real and demands repentance. But who of us is without sin? Who of us can claim any moral superiority or look down upon any of God's creatures? No, our motherhood must be compassionate, after the example of the Mother of Compassion who bore her seven sorrows.

In our pastoral openness to all, we must welcome back to the family of the Church any of our membership who have strayed so far as to willingly destroy human life. And we must recognize that within ourselves we have the potential to do likewise if we do not turn ourselves over completely to God's grace and the Spirit's guidance.

"By their love you will know them."

Mother Mary, guide the growth of the Church. Teach it your way of prayer and faithfulness. Inspire us to live the Gospel as you did, loyal to the Christ and conforming our life to his. Comforter of the afflicted, from your place in heaven, pray for us sinners now and at the hour of our death.

QUESTIONS FOR REFLECTION

....

The doctrine of the Assumption demonstrates Mary's unique and privileged place in the Communion of Saints. How has Mary ever helped you to make a complete and sincere Fiat ("Yes") to God's will?

Matter is to be reverenced. For this reason, the remains of the deceased, cremated or not, are to be buried in the ground. How does reverence for the earth translate into respecting our bodies?

Life is not something humans have fashioned as much as it is a gift from God. It is to be respected. What is your experience promoting this principle or working with people who observe or violate it?

The Crowning of Mary:
My Mother, My Queen

"Mary, my mother, my queen!"

Patrick Peyton, C.S.C.

When Servant of God Patrick Peyton, C.S.C., was dying, his very last words were these: "Mary, my mother, my queen!" This dedicated, holy priest had served Mary for his whole priesthood. He was totally focused on promoting the family Rosary, and the message was well received. Father Peyton preached all around the world the strengthening of families through family Rosary prayer together. Recently, a study by the National Marriage Project at the University of Virginia indicated a correlation between prayer together and the happiness of married couples. Truly, the family that prays together does stay together; the research bears out what Father Peyton has said for decades!

Father Peyton understood that Mary is our mother and that prayer with our mother keeps families together. But he also called Mary his "queen." Why does the Church refer to Mary as royalty? What does this reference really mean? These questions were answered for me when I visited Uganda (in eastern Africa) and was preparing to give a talk on Mary and Father Peyton's work to the members of a parish in Kampala. The pastor, as he went to the pulpit to introduce me, thought I should understand a little about the parish's history. "Because of where this parish is and how it originated, the parishioners here know Our Lady well, and understand who she is as queen," he said.

I listened carefully as the pastor explained that the parish was called, in the local language (Luganda), "I Saw You" parish. I found this name very unusual and listened all the more carefully. "You see," the pastor continued, "this property was the property of the local King, and it was forbidden for anyone to trespass on the King's property. There were guards posted, and if someone was caught trespassing, they captured him and brought him before the King to be judged and sentenced. 'I saw you!' was their accusation. 'I saw you trespass on the royal property, and this is forbidden under pain of death!' The King would be likely to convict the offender on the spot and order that he be killed in the King's presence. We have a cemetery on the property still today filled with trespassers and other offenders.

"And the only one who could change the King's mind was the Queen Mother! The Queen was always the mother of the King, and if she knew the family of the accused, they would run to her to ask her intercession. Whatever the Queen requested would be heeded by her son, the King, out of gratitude and love toward her. So if the Queen asked for leniency, the sentence would be commuted and a life would be saved.

"We know Mary to be the Queen Mother of the King, Jesus Christ. We know to go to her and ask her intercession with her Son. How could he refuse the mother he loves? The King will do what the Queen Mother requests. We go to her often. Mary is our friend and confidante, our Queen."

This encounter in Africa gave me a better sense of what is meant by the queenship of Mary. I have always considered her to be the first among the saints, the first disciple. She knew her Son better than anyone else. She is mother to the Church as well as mother to Jesus. Mary has great concern for all of us, especially the poor, the dispossessed, the destitute, and children. She has appeared over the centuries to the humble, who needed her the most. Given to us at the foot of the cross as Mother, Mary is elevated to Queen Mother after her assumption into heaven. The Queen Mother will intercede with her Son and tell the servants, the angels, to "do whatever he tells you!" As Father Peyton said, as much in his life as in his dying: "Mary, my mother; my queen!"

If Jesus spent his public years on this earth preaching and teaching about the nature of the Kingdom of God, as these Rosary mysteries suggest (especially the third Luminous Mystery), then this Kingdom has a queen, and she is Mary. Father Peyton was well aware of the intercession of Mary, whom tradition calls "omnipotent by grace." In other words, as Father Con Haggerty, C.S.C., had explained to Pat Peyton, the seminarian, as he suffered with life-threatening tuberculosis, "Mary is a 100 percenter! If 25 percent or 50 percent is all you believe you will receive from her, then that's all you deserve. You have to believe that she can give you 100 percent of what you ask only by the power and grace of Jesus Christ, who will refuse her nothing." Pat believed; he prayed his Rosary with all his heart, and he was healed by God's grace and guided by Mary to become the American Apostle of the Rosary! (Cardinal Spellman of New York gave him this title in 1945.) Such a powerful, compassionate queen!

What would you like to be most remembered for? What could be the crowning achievement of your life? The comic actor W. C. Fields is said to have suggested this epitaph, or something similar, for his gravestone: "Frankly, I'd rather be in Philadelphia!" My father used to joke that he would like to have his gravestone epitaph read: "At least it hasn't been dull!"

An appropriate epitaph for Mary is her Magnificat: "My soul proclaims the greatness of the Lord; my spirit rejoices in God, my Savior. For he has looked upon his handmaid's lowliness. Behold, from now on will all ages call me blessed. The Mighty One has done great things for me, and holy is his name. . . ." This is a prayer, a hymn we could all pray. A life in which Jesus is our King and Mary our Queen cannot go wrong, for they give purpose to our life. The simple prayer of the Rosary puts all of this in mind. It helps us retrace the most important events in the life of Jesus Christ, a life that we seek to imitate: the birth of the Son of God among us by Mary's participation; his proclamation of the Kingdom of God by teaching and example; his suffering and death, which redeemed us; and the overshadowing of the Holy Spirit upon the ancient church after his resurrection and ascension.

These holy mysteries happen today in our lives as well if we can only recognize them. Every birth among us brings another "child of the promise" who can reveal who Christ is for us; every act of forgiveness by us or toward us helps define the Kingdom; every cross we bear in life puts us in mind of the sinless one who bore the cross for us; every inspiration we receive to reach out in service to others and thereby evangelize is a little Pentecost.

May you pray the Rosary, especially together with your family, in a manner that opens your eyes to the many ways our lives can reflect Christ's life. May you and your family be strengthened by the faithful practice of not only praying the Rosary, but living the Rosary together and finding your lives in the mysteries.

QUESTIONS FOR REFLECTION

When has Our Lady ever interceded for you as the Queen Mother? Explain.

Mary stood by the cross and maintained her hope. How has she, as a human being who has suffered as we have, inspired you to find hope even in the cross?

What great things has the Almighty done for you? How have you shared this with others?

Appendix:
How to Pray the Rosary

What Is the Rosary?

THE BASICS

The Rosary is a meditative prayer that recalls the lives of Jesus and Mary. It is normally prayed with Rosary beads. Rosary beads come in many shapes and sizes, but typically they are a circular string of beads, often connected by a small medal to a string of five more beads and a cross. Praying the Rosary starts with the cross and moves up through the beads. Each bead is held in one's fingers, one at a time, and a standard prayer is prayed, such as the Apostles' Creed, the Our Father, the Hail Mary, the Doxology (the Glory Be), and the Hail Holy Queen.

The circular string of beads is divided into five *decades*. These five decades, when prayed together, make up what is called a "set of mysteries" of the Rosary. There are four sets of Rosary mysteries in all. Each mystery represents an event from the life of Jesus or Mary which is meditated upon the praying of each decade of the Rosary. The names of these four sets of mysteries are the *Joyful* Mysteries, the *Luminous* Mysteries, the *Sorrowful* Mysteries, and the *Glorious* Mysteries.

The Mysteries

The Joyful Mysteries

The Joyful Mysteries remind us of the joy of the incarnation. In the coming of Jesus Christ through the power of the Holy Spirit and the willingness of the Virgin Mary, God has come to be with his people. The Joyful Mysteries are:

The Annunciation
The Visitation
The Nativity
The Presentation
The Finding in the Temple

The Luminous Mysteries

The Luminous Mysteries recall the great events in the public ministry of Jesus, as he came to teach, to heal, and to give the gift of himself. These mysteries are:

The Baptism of Jesus in the Jordan by
  John the Baptist
The Wedding Feast at Cana
The Proclamation of the Kingdom

The Transfiguration
The Institution of the Eucharist

The Sorrowful Mysteries

The Sorrowful Mysteries focus on the great love our Lord had for us as seen in his passion and death. These mysteries are:

The Agony in the Garden
The Scourging at the Pillar
The Crowning with Thorns
The Carrying of the Cross
The Crucifixion

The Glorious Mysteries

The Glorious Mysteries recall the completion of the paschal mystery, from Jesus' triumph over death to his ascension and the birth of the Church. These mysteries are:

The Resurrection
The Ascension
Pentecost: The Coming of the Holy Spirit
The Assumption
The Crowning of Mary

Praying the Rosary

....

1. After deciding which mystery you wish to pray, take up your Rosary beads. Holding the cross in your right hand, make the Sign of the Cross and pray the Apostles' Creed, which summarizes the core beliefs we share as Catholics.

2. Each bead on the Rosary represents a prayer we pray. On the first large bead, the one right above the cross, pray the Our Father, the prayer Jesus taught us.

3. On each of the following three smaller beads, pray the Hail Mary. Then pray the doxology, more commonly known as the Glory Be.

4. On the space before the next bead, announce the set of mysteries you have chosen to pray (joyful, luminous, sorrowful, or glorious). Reflect on what happened to Jesus in these mysteries, and think about what they mean in your life today.

5. Announce the first mystery (for example, the Annunciation) and pray the Our Father on the next bead. Pray one Hail Mary for each of the next ten beads. Finish the mystery by praying the Glory Be either on the last of the ten beads or on the next large bead.

6. On the next large bead, announce the second mystery. Reflect, pray the Our Father, the ten Hail Marys, and finish again with the Glory Be. This continues until all five mysteries are completed.

7. When you have reached the end of the fifth decade, you may pray the Hail Holy Queen while holding the medal that connects the beads.

The Prayers of the Rosary

The following prayers are used while praying the Rosary:

APOSTLES' CREED

I believe in God, the Father Almighty, Creator of heaven and earth; and in Jesus Christ, His only Son, our Lord, who was conceived by the Holy Spirit, born of the Virgin Mary, suffered under Pontius Pilate, was crucified, died, and was buried. He descended to the dead; on the third day he rose again from the dead; he ascended into heaven, is seated at the right hand of God the Father Almighty; from thence he shall come to judge the living and the dead. I believe in the Holy Spirit, the Holy Catholic Church, the communion of Saints, the forgiveness of sins, the resurrection of the body, and life everlasting. Amen.

OUR FATHER

Our Father, who art in heaven, hallowed be thy name. Thy Kingdom come. Thy will be done on earth as it is in heaven. Give us this day our daily bread, and forgive us our trespasses as we forgive those who trespass against us; and lead us not into temptation, but deliver us from evil. Amen.

HAIL MARY

Hail Mary, full of Grace, the Lord is with thee. Blessed art thou among women, and blessed is the fruit of thy womb, Jesus. Holy Mary, Mother of God, pray for us sinners now and at the hour of our death. Amen.

DOXOLOGY, OR GLORY BE

Glory be to the Father and to the Son and to the Holy Spirit. As it was in the beginning is now and ever shall be, world without end. Amen.

HAIL HOLY QUEEN

Hail, Holy Queen, Mother of Mercy, our life, our sweetness, and our hope. To thee do we cry, poor banished children of Eve. To thee do we send up our sighs, mourning and weeping in this valley of tears. Turn then, O most gracious advocate, thine eyes of mercy toward us, and after this, our exile, show unto us the blessed fruit of thy womb, Jesus. O clement! O loving! O sweet Virgin Mary! Pray for us, O Holy Mother of God, that we may be made worthy of the promises of Christ.